Welcome to Table Talk

Table Talk helps children and adults explore the Bible together. Each day provides a short family Bible time which, with your own adaptation, could work for ages 4 to 12. It includes optional follow on material which takes the passage further for older children. There are also suggestions for linking **Table Talk** with **XTB** children's notes.

Who can use Table Talk?

- **Families**
- **One adult with one child**
- **A teenager with a younger brother or sister**
- **Children's leaders with their groups**
- **Any other mix that works for you!**

TableTalk
A short family Bible time for daily use. Table Talk takes about five minutes, maybe at breakfast, or after an evening meal. Choose whatever time and place suits you best as a family. Table Talk includes a simple discussion starter or activity that leads into a short Bible reading. This is followed by a few questions.

XTB
XTB children's notes help 7-11 year olds to get into the Bible for themselves. They are based on the same Bible passages as **Table Talk**. You will find suggestions for how **XTB** can be used alongside **Table Talk** on the next page.

In the next three pages you'll find suggestions for how to use Table Talk, along with hints and tips for adapting it to your own situation. If you've never done anything like this before, check out our web page for further help (go to www.thegoodbook.co.uk and click on Daily Reading) or write in for a fact sheet.

THE SMALL PRINT

Table Talk is published by The Good Book Company, 37 Elm Road, New Malden, Surrey, KT3 3HB
Tel: 02089420880. www.thegoodbook.co.uk. Written by Alison Mitchell. email: Alison@thegoodbook.co.uk
Fab pictures by Kirsty McAllister. Bible quotations taken from The Good News Bible.
AUSTRALIA: Distributed by Matthias Media. Tel: (02) 9663 1478; email: info@matthiasmedia.com.au

HOW TO USE Table Talk

Table Talk is designed to last for up to three months. How you use it depends on what works for you. We have included 60 full days of material in this issue, plus some more low-key suggestions for another 30 days (see page 45). We would like to encourage you to work establishing a pattern of family reading. The first two weeks are the hardest!

Table Talk is based on the same Bible passages as *XTB*, but usually only asks for two or three verses to be read out loud. The full *XTB* passage is listed at the top of each **Table Talk** page. If you are using **Table Talk** with older children, read the full *XTB* passage rather than the shorter version.

KEYPOINT
This is the main point you should be trying to convey. Don't read this out—it often gives away the end of the story!

The main part of **Table Talk** is designed to be suitable for younger children. Building Up includes more difficult questions designed for older children, or those with more Bible knowledge.

As far as possible, if your children are old enough to read the Bible verses for themselves, encourage them to find the answers in the passage and to tell you which verse the answer is in. This will help them to get used to handling the Bible for themselves.

The **Building Up** section is designed to build on the passage studied in Table Talk (and XTB). Building Up includes some additional questions which reinforce the main teaching point, apply the teaching more directly or follow up any difficult issues raised by the passage.

Linking with *XTB*

The **XTB** children's notes are based on the same passages as **Table Talk**. There are a number of ways in which you can link the two together:
- Children do **XTB** on their own. Parents then follow these up later (see suggestions below).
- A child and adult work through **XTB** together.
- A family uses **Table Talk** together at breakfast. Older children then use **XTB** on their own later.
- You use **Table Talk** on its own, with no link to **XTB**.

FOLLOWING UP XTB

If your child uses **XTB** on their own it can be helpful to ask them later to show you (or tell you) what they've done. Some useful starter questions are:

- Can you tell me what the reading was about?

- Did anything surprise you in the reading? Was there anything that would have surprised the people who first saw it or read about it?

- Is there anything you didn't understand or want to ask about?

- What did you learn about God, Jesus or the Holy Spirit?

- Is there anything you're going to do as a result of reading this passage?

- Did you stick in a Promise sticker? If so, why? What was the promise?

Table Talk is deliberately not too ambitious. Most families find it quite hard to set up a regular pattern of reading the Bible together—and when they do meet, time is often short. So **Table Talk** is designed to be quick and easy to use, needing little in the way of extra materials, apart from pen and paper now and then.

BUT!!

Most families have special times when they **can** be more ambitious, or do have some extra time available. Here are some suggestions for how you can use **Table Talk** as the basis for a special family adventure...

PICNIC
Take Table Talk with you on a family picnic. Thank God for His beautiful Creation.

WALK
Go for a walk together. Stop somewhere with a good view and read Genesis 1v1—2v4.

GETTING TOGETHER
Invite another family for a meal, and to read the Bible together. The children could make a poster based on the passage.

MUSEUM
Visit a museum to see a display from Bible times. Use it to remind yourselves that the Bible tells us about real people and real history.

HOLIDAYS
Set aside a special time each day while on holiday. Choose some unusual places to read the Bible together—on the beach, up a mountain, in a boat... Take some photos to put on your Tale Talk display when you get back from holiday.

You could try one of the special holiday editions of XTB and Table Talk—**Christmas Unpacked, Easter Unscrambled** and **Summer Signposts**.

Have an adventure!

FOOD!
Eat some food linked with the passage you are studying. For example Manna (biscuits made with honey, Exodus 16v31), Unleavened bread or Honeycomb (Matthew 3v4— but don't try the locusts!)

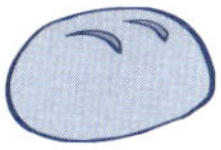

DISPLAY AREA
We find it easier to remember and understand what we learn when we have something to look at. Make a Table Talk display area, for pictures, Bible verses and prayers. Add to it regularly.

VIDEO
A wide range of Bible videos are available—from simple cartoon stories, to whole Gospels filmed with real life actors. (Your local Christian bookshop should have a range.) Choose one that ties in with the passages you are reading together. _Note:_ Use the video **in addition** to the Bible passage, not **instead** of it!

PRAYER DIARY
As a special project, make a family prayer diary. Use it to keep a note of things you pray for—and the answers God gives you. This can be a tremendous help to children (and parents!) to learn to trust God in prayer as we see how he answers over time.

Go on—try it!

DRAMA OR PUPPETS
Take time to dramatise a Bible story. Maybe act it out (with costumes if possible) or make some simple puppets to retell the story.

Enough of the introduction, let's get going...

DAYS 1-15
Notes for Parents

THE BOOK OF ACTS
Acts is the second book written by a doctor called Luke. His first book tells the life of Jesus. His second book tells us what happened after Jesus died and came back to life again.

Acts is short for "Acts of the Apostles". It's all about how Jesus' closest disciples (now called apostles) began to spread the good news about Jesus.

Note: *Disciple* means "pupil" or "learner". It is used in the Gospels to describe all those who followed Jesus. In practice, we often use this title for Jesus' twelve closest followers. *Apostle* means "sent one". The twelve Apostles were chosen (sent) by Jesus to tell the world about Him. (Acts 1v8)

THE HOLY SPIRIT FACT BOX
It is important to make clear to people that the Holy Spirit isn't a force (like electricity). He's a **person**. He's **God**! Jesus sends us His Spirit to live inside us and help us to follow Him.

THE HELPER
The Holy Spirit helps us
★ wherever we are
★ to know Jesus is with us
★ to follow Jesus
★ to tell others about Jesus
★ to pray

Always refer to Him as *He* not it. Some children can be worried about the Spirit (associations with ghosts/spirits etc.). Make sure they understand that He is the Spirit of *Jesus* with the same character as the Lord—powerful, but also loving, kind, caring.

Children may like to make or draw a Fact Box, or design one on a computer, to put these facts in. Extra information can be added as you read through the Book of

DAY 1 The never-ending story

KEYPOINT
Jesus tells His followers to wait for the Holy Spirit, who will help them to follow Jesus

Today's passages are:
Table Talk: Acts 1v4-5
XTB: Acts 1v1-5

 Luke wrote two books—Luke's Gospel and Acts. (Gospel means "Good News".) In his Gospel, Luke *"wrote about all that Jesus began to do and teach until the day he was taken up to heaven"* (Acts 1v1-2). Think of **five** things Luke would have written about *or* flick through Luke's Gospel to find some examples.

 Luke's second book, Acts, tells us what happened after Jesus died and came back to life. It starts with Jesus telling His followers to *wait*... **Read Acts 1v4-5**

 What did Jesus tell His friends to wait for?—v4 (*The gift that God His Father promised*) What was this gift?—v5 (*The Holy Spirit*) The Holy Spirit is called "The Helper". Why do you think that is? How does He help us? Read the *Holy Spirit Fact Box* in **Notes for Parents** to find out more.

 The Holy Spirit helped Jesus' friends to keep following Him—and to tell others about Him. Following Jesus is hard at times. We need help too.

 Ask God to help you—even when it's hard.

Building up
After being brought back to life, Jesus spent 40 days with His followers. **Read Acts 1v3** to see what Jesus did and taught during that time. Why do you think Jesus' followers needed proof that He really was alive? How would this help them later, when they started to tell other people about Him?

DAY 2 Mission impossible?

KEYPOINT
The Holy Spirit will help Jesus' followers to spread the message about Him.

Today's passages are:
Table Talk: Acts 1v8
XTB: Acts 1v6-11

 I live near London. How many ways could you get a message to me? (*Post, phone, visit, email, text message, fax, messenger...*)

 Jesus' followers had to tell other people the great message about Jesus. How many people do you think they had to tell? **Read Acts 1v8** to see what Jesus said.

 What four places does Jesus mention? Who would help them to witness (tell people) about Jesus? (*The Holy Spirit*)

(*Optional*) Find Israel and **Jerusalem** in an atlas. **Judea** and **Samaria** are both parts of modern Israel. Look for countries nearby where the message about Jesus could spread quickly. Now find some far away countries—"**the ends of the earth**".

A bunch of ordinary men telling the whole world about Jesus seems an impossible mission! *Why wasn't it?*

 The good news about Jesus has spread to every country in the world. It has reached **you** too! Thank God for the people who tell you about Jesus.

Building up
Find out how Jesus left His disciples by reading **Acts 1v9-11**. Film makers use special effects to make people appear to float, but Jesus really did rise up into the air! *Why do you think Jesus was able do this?* The angels promised that Jesus would come back again. *Are you looking forward to Jesus returning? Why?*

DAY 3 The Chatterbox team

KEYPOINT
Matthias is chosen to replace Judas. The Holy Spirit will help him to tell others about Jesus.

Today's passages are:
Table Talk: Acts 1v21-22 + 26
XTB: Acts 1v21-26

 Are any of you chatterboxes? (i.e. You can't stop talking!) The apostles were to be chatterboxes about **Jesus**—but they needed one more man to join them. What kind of man do you think they'd need? (*What might he be good at? What would he need to know?*)

 Peter described the kind of man they needed. **Read Acts 1v21-22**

What did Peter say was most important? (*Someone who'd been with Jesus from the beginning.*) What are some of the things this man would have seen and heard? (*Miracles, Jesus' teaching, Jesus' death and resurrection...*)

Read v26 to find out who was chosen. This was a H-U-G-E job. Who would help Matthias to do it? (*Holy Spirit, 1v8*)

 Who do you know who tells other people about Jesus? Ask God to help them.

Building up
A twelfth apostle was needed to replace Judas. The Old T had said that one of Jesus' followers would betray Him, and that he must be replaced. Read Peter's summary of this in **Acts 1v15-17 + v20**. Think about the qualifications Peter didn't include in v21-22 (e.g. good at making speeches, clever, brave...) Why didn't Peter add any of these? What's most important for people **today** if they're going to tell others about Jesus?

DAY 4
Great tongues of fire!

KEYPOINT
Jesus keeps His promise to send the Holy Spirit.

Today's passages are:
Table Talk: Acts 2v1-4
XTB: Acts 2v1-4

TABLE TALK

How many languages can you speak? (Even if it's just to say **Yes**, **No** or **Hello**!) How about **Hebrew**? (Oh yes, you do! Alleluia [Hallelu Yah] is Hebrew. It means **Praise the Lord**.)

READ

Jesus had promised that the Holy Spirit would come. He did—with some very surprising results! **Read Acts 2v1-4**

TALK

What three strange things happened? (v2—sound of wind, v3—tongues of fire, v4—other languages) Jesus' followers were to be chatterboxes about Him. When the Holy Spirit came He gave them new languages. How would they help?

PRAY

Praise God in these different languages—they all mean "Praise the Lord."
Le Seigneur soit loué! (French)
Looft den Here! (Dutch)
Il Signore sia lodato! (Italian)
El Señor sea glorificado! (Spanish)

DO

(Optional) Make a poster praising God in these languages. Include English and Hebrew too. You could draw flags as well.

Building up
The apostles had the task of telling others about Jesus. Some of them also wrote the books that make up the New T. But what if they <u>forgot</u> some of what they had seen or heard? Or didn't <u>understand</u> it? **Read John 14v25-26** to see how the Holy Spirit helped them. Thank God for making sure that what the apostles taught and wrote down about Jesus was true and accurate.

DAY 5
Look who's talking

KEYPOINT
The Spirit gives Jesus' followers new languages to help them spread the message.

Today's passages are:
Table Talk: Acts 2v5-8
XTB: Acts 2v5-13

TABLE TALK

<u>Either</u>: Use an atlas to find Israel, Turkey, Crete, Egypt and Italy. <u>Or</u>: Give clues to guess some of these places.

READ

Remind each other of yesterday's story. Pentecost was a Jewish harvest festival, so there were loads of people in Jerusalem for the celebrations. They came from many countries, including the ones listed above. **Read Acts 2v5-8**

TALK

Why did the crowd gather? (v6) (They heard the noise.) What surprised them so much? (Galileans, from North Israel, spoke in all their languages.) **Read v8 again.** How would you answer their question?

PRAY

God wants the <u>whole world</u> to hear about Jesus. Pray for anyone you know who teaches about Jesus in another country. If you can, send them an email, letter or gift and tell them you are praying for them.

Building up
God could have sent the Spirit at any time. Why do you think He chose a time when so many people were visiting Jerusalem? **Read Acts 2v12-13** to see two reactions to what happened. Have **you** told anyone about Jesus recently? How did they react? Were they amazed? Or puzzled? Did they laugh at you? Talk about the best way to respond to these different reactions. Ask God to help you to keep talking to others about Jesus.

DAY 6
Peter pipes up

KEYPOINT
Peter tells the crowds that Jesus is the Christ (God's chosen King)—but that they killed Him!

Today's passages are:
Table Talk: Acts 2v17,23,24,31,33
XTB: Acts 2v14-36

TABLE TALK
Copy these five sentences onto strips of paper. These are the key parts of Peter's speech to the crowds in Acts 2. Try to put them into the correct order.

DO

A: God brought Jesus back to life.
B: Jesus has poured out His Spirit on His followers.
C: Long ago God said amazing things would happen when He sent the Holy Spirit.
D: Jesus is the Christ (*God's chosen King*).
E: It was always God's plan that Jesus would be killed.

READ
Check **Acts 2 vs 17, 23, 24, 31 + 33** to see what order Peter said these in. (*Answer: CEADB*) Note: Keep this list for tomorrow's Table Talk.

THINK
Peter has just told the crowds that Jesus is the **promised King**—but that they killed Him! How do you think they will react? (*More about that tomorrow.*)

PRAY
Look again at the five points listed. Notice how God was always in control. Praise God that His plans always work out.

Building up
When Peter was talking to the crowd, he summed up some key facts about Jesus. **Read Acts 2v22-24.** Find at least <u>five</u> important facts about Jesus in the verses. Verse 23 says that Jesus was killed by **men**—but that it was always part of **God's** plan. Who was in control?

Does v24 confirm your answer?

DAY 1-15
Notes for Parents

GOD'S RESCUE PLAN
(*You need pencil & paper.*) *Prepare three separate pieces of paper. Write* **GOD** *on one,* **SIN** *on a second, and draw a person (a stick man is fine) on the third.*

Place the pieces of paper as shown.

ASK: WHAT IS SIN?
Sin is more than just doing wrong things. We all like to be **in charge** of our own lives. We do what **we** want instead of what **God** wants. This is called Sin.

ASK: WHAT DOES SIN DO?
As the picture shows, **sin** gets in the way between us and God. It stops us from knowing God and from being His friends. Sin is a H-U-G-E problem—and there is nothing **we** can do about it.

In **Acts 2v38** Peter says that our sins can be forgiven. This isn't because of anything **we** do—but because of what **Jesus** did. When Jesus died on the cross He was being punished. He took the punishment that we deserve, so that we can be forgiven.

Take the paper saying SIN and tear it in half. Then place the two halves as shown.

ASK: WHAT GETS IN THE WAY NOW BETWEEN PEOPLE AND GOD?
(*Answer: Nothing!*)
When Jesus died, He dealt with the problem of sin so that we can be forgiven. There is nothing to separate us from God any more. This was **God's Rescue Plan** for us.

DAY 7
What shall we do?

KEYPOINT
Peter tells the crowds to repent—to turn away from their sins. We need to repent too.

Today's passages are:
Table Talk: Acts 2v38-39
XTB: Acts 2v37-40

 TABLE TALK — **Recap:** Look again at yesterday's five points from Peter's speech.

 **READ** — When the people heard Peter's speech, they asked, "What shall we do?" **Read Acts 2v38-39**

 TALK — Peter told them to **repent**. What does that mean? (*To repent doesn't just mean saying sorry. It means asking God to help you to change, and to do what He says.*) What two things did Peter say would happen? (*Their sins will be forgiven, they'll be given the gift of the Holy Spirit.*)

 **DO** — Use the illustration in **Notes for Parents** (*on the previous page*) to show how Jesus rescues us from our sins.

 PRAY — Verse 39 means that this promise is for **us** too—even though we live 2000 years after Peter! Thank God for sending Jesus so that you can be forgiven.

Building up
Peter told people to "repent and be baptised". At that time, trusting Jesus and getting baptised happened together. The baptism was a public sign that someone had put their faith in Jesus and was now living for Him. Why does it help to make a public stand for your faith? Do people know that **you** are a Christian? How?

DAY 8
Growing all the time

KEYPOINT
About 3000 people became followers of Jesus. These new Christians had changed lives.

Today's passages are:
Table Talk: Acts 2v45-47
XTB: Acts 2v41-47

 TABLE TALK — Do any of you have a nickname? Would you like one—and if so, what? The first followers of Jesus were given a nickname—**Christians**. Why do you think they were called that? (*They believed Jesus was the **Christ**, which means **God's chosen King**.*)

 **READ** — After hearing Peter's speech, about 3000 people became followers of Jesus—**Christians**. (v41) They met together every day. Read what they were like in **Acts 2v45-47**

 **TALK** — What did these new Christians do? (*Shared with each other, gave to those in need, met daily, praised God.*) What did others think of them? (*See v47*)

 **THINK** — If someone looked at **your** life, could they tell that you are a Christian? How? If not, what needs to change?

 **PRAY** — Ask God to help you to live for Him, just as these early believers did.

Building up
Read Acts 2v44-45
Think carefully about **your** money and possessions. How do you decide the best way to use them? Think of someone you know who has less than you. How can you share with them? Ask God to help you to do it.

DAY 9 The three o'clock miracle

KEYPOINT
Peter heals a lame man in the name of Jesus.

Today's passages are:
Table Talk: Acts 3v1-8
XTB: Acts 3v1-10

 (*Preparation*) Write WHO, WHAT, WHERE, WHEN, and WHY on five pieces of paper.

 **Read Acts 3v1-8** Younger children may like to act the story out, to mime it as you read it again, or to retell it using dolls or puppets.

 Use the question cards to talk about the story.

WHO was there? (*Peter, John, lame man*). **WHERE** were they? (*Temple, Beautiful gate*). **WHEN** did it happen? (*3 o'clock in the afternoon—the "ninth hour"*). **WHAT** happened? (*retell the main points— beginning, middle and end*). **WHY** was the man "walking, jumping and praising God" (v8)?

This man was very excited! He easily could have forgotten to thank God—but he didn't! It's easy to forget to thank God for the great things He has given us. Think of some things to thank and praise God for now.

Building up
A good way to help you understand a Bible passage is to ask questions. **WHY** is particularly useful. *For example:* **Why** were Peter and John going to the Temple? (v1) **Why** did Peter say what he did to the lame man? (v6) **Why** was Peter able to heal the man? **Why** do you think Luke included this story in the book of Acts?

DAY 10 Chatterbox time

KEYPOINT
The crowds thought *Peter* had healed the lame man—but he points them to *Jesus*.

Today's passages are:
Table Talk: Acts 3v12 + 16
XTB: Acts 3v11-16

 Have some fun asking each other questions. Every answer has to include **Banana**! e.g. How are you going to school? *On my banana.* What's the weather like? *It's raining cats and bananas!*

 The crowds were **amazed** by the healing of the lame man. They thought Peter must be special and powerful—but Peter said not! **Read Acts 3v12** Why didn't Peter want them to think he'd healed the man by his own power? What do you think Peter will talk about now? (*No—it's not bananas!*)

 **Read Acts 3v16** Who does Peter talk about <u>instead</u> of himself? What does he say about Jesus?

 Peter took every opportunity to be a chatterbox about Jesus. Do you? What opportunities will you have this week to tell someone about Jesus? Ask God to help you.

Building up
Read Acts 3v13-15 We saw yesterday how asking questions helps us to understand a Bible passage more clearly. *Here's a few more:*

The crowds were amazed by the *miracle*, but **What** does Peter choose to talk about? Use these verses to make two lists. 1—What does Peter say that **God** has done? 2—What had the **people** done? **Why** did Peter want them to know all this? **Why** did Peter say that the apostles are witnesses (v15)? (*To show it's true.*)

DAY 11
Signposts

KEYPOINT
Miracles are like signposts, pointing to who Jesus is.

Today's passages are:
Table Talk: Acts 3v16
XTB: Acts 3v16

 TABLE TALK
Where might you see a **"Keep Out!"** sign? Or a **"Welcome"** sign? What are they for?

 **READ**
John's Gospel says that miracles are like **signposts** (John 20v31). Jesus' miracles point to <u>who Jesus is.</u> Peter's miracle was like a signpost too. **Read Acts 3v16**

 **TALK**
Who did Peter's miracle point to? (*Jesus*) How was this man healed? (*By faith in the name of Jesus.*) Is Peter saying this man was healed by faith in a <u>dead</u> man? (*No! God brought Jesus back to life—v15*)

 **THINK**
Jesus didn't die a second time—He is still alive today. We can't see Him or touch Him, but we can know that He is with us. Jesus sends us His Spirit to live inside us and help us to follow Him.

 PRAY
Dear Jesus, thank you that You are still alive today. Please help us to follow You today and always. Amen

Building up
Have fun chasing down some other verses that end in 3v16.

John 3v16 is probably the best known verse in the Bible. How does it link with **Acts 3v16**? Compare these verses with **1 John 3v16** and **Matthew 3v16-17**. What do all these verses have in common? Finally check out **2 Timothy 3v16** (*This explains why Table Talk aims to help you to read the Bible for yourself.*)

DAY 12
Notes for Parents

PROMISED LONG AGO...
The crowd Peter was speaking to were Jewish. They would have known their Old Testament very well—the **people** in it and the **promises** God made...

MOSES
God promised that He would send a prophet (which means God's messenger) like **Moses**. The people must listen to this new prophet. (*This promise is in Deuteronomy 18v15 + 18*)

THE PROPHETS
The Old Testament **prophets** spoke of a time when God would send a **rescuer** to His people, called the Messiah or Christ. (*For example, in Isaiah 53v4-6, and Zechariah 9v9.*)

ABRAHAM
God promised that one of **Abraham's** family would be God's way of blessing the whole world. (*See Genesis 12v3 + 22v18*)

In the last part of his speech, Peter showed that **Jesus** came as the answer to <u>all three promises</u>. **Read Acts 3v22-26**

Wow! God promised that Jesus would come—and He did! He came to rescue His people and bless the whole world—just as God had said. We can trust God to **always** do what He says.

DAY 12
Promised long ago

KEYPOINT
Peter tells the crowds to turn away from sin, and turn towards God.

Today's passages are:
Table Talk: Acts 3v19
XTB: Acts 3v17-26

TABLE TALK

Note: *The end of Peter's speech is quite complex. Older children may like to follow it through using **Notes for Parents** on the previous page. With younger children just focus on verse 19.*

Do you remember what Peter told people to do at the end of his last speech? (*Acts 2v38—"Repent and be baptised."*) What do you think he will tell people to do at the end of this speech?

READ

This time Peter tells the crowd something to **turn away** from and something to **turn towards**. **Read Acts 3v19**

TALK

What are they to turn away from? (*Sin*)
What are they to turn towards? (*God*)

Last time 3000 people became Christians. (Acts 2v41) What do you think will happen this time?
Read Acts 4v4 to find out.

PRAY

Wow! Loads of people believed the message about Jesus, and turned to God. Thank God for anyone **you** know who has become a follower of Jesus recently.

Building up
See **Notes for Parents** (left) for ideas on how to build on today's **Table Talk**.

DAY 13
B-I-G trouble!

KEYPOINT
The Holy Spirit helped Peter to keep bravely talking about Jesus, even when it got him into trouble

Today's passages are:
Table Talk: Acts 4v7-10
XTB: Acts 4v1-12

TABLE TALK

Play two quick games of hangman. The words are **Chatterbox** and **Prison**.

READ

Because he was a chatterbox about Jesus, Peter got into BIG trouble. The Temple leaders had Peter and John thrown into prison! The next morning they were dragged in front of the Jewish Council.
Read Acts 4v7-10

TALK

What question was Peter asked? (v7) What was his answer? (v10) The men questioning Peter were the same ones who had Jesus **killed**! Why was Peter able to answer them so bravely? (v8—*the Holy Spirit helped him.*)

THINK

Do your friends laugh at you for following Jesus? Or say that church is boring? The Holy Spirit will help you to stand up for Jesus—just as He helped Peter.

PRAY

Ask God to help you to stand up for Jesus.

Building up
Read Acts 4v11-12 Peter again shows how the Old Testament points forward to Jesus. (*He is quoting Psalm 118v22*) Why does Peter want the people to understand that the Old T talks about Jesus? (*The Jewish leaders claimed that Jesus had not come from God.*) You sometimes hear people say that all religions are the **same**. What does v12 say about that? Compare it with Jesus' own words in **John 14v6**.

DAY 14
Stop talking!

KEYPOINT
Peter knew that God had to come first—no matter what happened—so he carried on talking about Jesus.

Today's passages are:
Table Talk: Acts 4v18-20
XTB: Acts 4v13-22

Do you ever get told to stop talking? Why?

The Jewish leaders had a problem. They **hated** what Peter was saying about Jesus—but they couldn't pretend the miracle hadn't happened. So they decided to tell Peter & John to <u>stop</u> being chatterboxes! **Read Acts 4v18-20**

What were Peter & John told not to do? (*Not to speak or teach in the name of Jesus*) Did Peter agree to do what they said? (*No!*) Who was Peter going to obey instead? (*See v19*)

Peter knew that God had to come **first**—no matter what happened. When do **you** find it hard to put God first? (*e.g. when your friends want you to lie to get them out of trouble, or when you don't feel like reading your Bible or going to church.*)

PRAY
Ask God to help you to put Him first—just as He helped Peter & John.

Building up
Peter & John were ordinary men. They hadn't even had much schooling. So why were they able to stand up to these leaders so bravely, and explain themselves so clearly? Think about <u>your</u> answer to this question—then compare it with **Acts 4v13** to see what Luke wrote. Why do you think being with Jesus had made such a huge difference?

DAY 15
Growing all the time

KEYPOINT
The Holy Spirit helped Jesus' followers to be bold, and to keep spreading the message about Jesus.

Today's passages are:
Table Talk: Acts 4v29-31
XTB: Acts 4v23-31

Recap the whole story. Every time you mention **Peter** everyone has to stand up, turn around and sit down again. (**Key points:** *Peter & John [P&J] went to the Temple, healed lame man, crowds amazed, P spoke about Jesus, many believed, P&J arrested, P spoke about Jesus again, P&J set free but told <u>not</u> to speak about Jesus.*)

Peter & John were set free, and went back to the other believers. They'd been told **not** to speak about Jesus. Instead they asked God to help them **keep** talking about Him!
Read Acts 4v29-31

What did they ask God for? (*v29—help to speak <u>boldly</u> about Jesus, v30—miracles*) The believers wanted **everyone** to know about Jesus. That's why they asked God for help. How did God answer their prayer? (*v31*)

If we ask God to help us tell others about Jesus, He will **always** help us. Pray to Him now—thanking Him and asking for His help.

Building up
Look back through the first four chapter of **Acts**. What have you found out about the first Christians? Can you think of some ways that <u>you</u> are like those early believers? How could you be <u>more</u> like them? Pray together about your answers.

DAYS 16-30
Notes for Parents

THE BOOK OF GENESIS
Genesis is a Greek word. It means **"beginnings"**. The book of Genesis is a book of beginnings. It tells us about:

- The beginning of the **universe**
- The beginning of the **human race**
- The beginning of God's special family, **the Israelites**

HOW? WHO? and WHY?
How we came to be here is a fiercely debated question among Christians (sometimes too fiercely)! Whatever your view on **How** the universe came into being, it is important to concentrate on teaching children **Who** made us and **Why**. And also why the world is in such a mess. These are questions that are at the heart of Genesis also (and which Christians have no disagreement about!) The major questions of life are answered in this remarkable book, so it is very important that you do not teach it as 'just another creation story.' (Your children will probably have been exposed to other creation stories at school already).

In Genesis we see what God is like. During the next fifteen days of Table Talk we will see that God is the **Star-Maker** and **Promise-Giver**. (Note: In the XTB children's notes, children stick in Promise stickers whenever God is shown to be making or keeping a promise.)

Genesis also shows that God is **King** of the world that He made. But sadly we see that people <u>don't want</u> God to be their King. (This is what **Sin** is.)

BLOW YOUR MIND!
The Bible starts with **God**. Nobody made God. Before anything else existed, God was already there! This is incredibly hard to get our heads around—but it's true!

DAY 16
In the beginning...

KEYPOINT
God created the Universe out of absolutely nothing. He just spoke—and it was made!

Today's passages are:
Table Talk: Genesis 1v1-5
XTB: Genesis 1v1-5

 **TABLE TALK**
Give everyone one minute to collect one or more things that give **light**. (e.g. torch, candle, bike light, table lamp—be careful with plugs... You could put things round the room beforehand.)

 **READ**
Today's reading starts at the very beginning of the Bible. It tells us where light came from...
Read Genesis 1v1-5

 **TALK**
Who is the first person mentioned in the Bible? (v1—God) What did God do? (He created everything) Verse 3 tells us that God created light. How did He make it? (He spoke)

 **DO**
(Optional) Ask your child to draw the sun. What did they need to draw it? (Paper, and a pen or pencil) Can they make a picture out of <u>nothing</u>? (No!) But God is **so powerful** that He created the universe out of absolutely nothing! He just <u>spoke</u>—and the universe was made!

 **THINK**
Imagine if there was **no light**—and everything was always dark. Think of some things you <u>couldn't</u> do.

 **PRAY**
Thank God for creating our world—and for the light to see and enjoy it.

Building up
The book of Genesis doesn't mention Jesus by name—but He's there. The New Testament makes it clear that Jesus is the Word through whom all things were made. Check out **John 1v1-3** and **Colossians 1v15-17**. What do these verses tell you about Jesus?

DAY 17   He also made the stars

KEYPOINT
Everything God made was good—it was just how God wanted it to be.

Today's passages are:
Table Talk: Genesis 1v24-25
XTB: Genesis 1v6-25

 TABLE TALK
Ask each person to choose a favourite animal—and to say why they chose it.

 **READ**
Chapter One of Genesis tells us the order in which God made things when He created the world. Use **Notes for Parents** (opposite) to check out what God made on Days 1 to 6.

Find out more about Day Six by reading **Genesis 1v24-25**

 **TALK**
How many kinds of animal did God make? (*Loads!*) Why do you think God made so many? Think of some words to describe what God made (*e.g. great, beautiful, varied...*) Genesis describes everything God made as **good**. It was just how God wanted it to be.

 PRAY
Each choose <u>two</u> things in Creation to thank God for. Take it in turns to pray: **Thank You God for making...**

Building up
Read **Genesis 1v16**

The end of v16 is my favourite throwaway line in the Bible: "He also made the stars." What does this great sentence tell you about God? Compare it with **Psalm 147v4**

There are further *Building Up* suggestions in **Notes for Parents** opposite.

DAY 17
Notes for Parents

THE DAYS OF CREATION

Day 1 (v3-5)	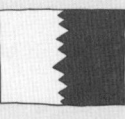	Day and night
Day 2 (v6-8)		Sky and water
Day 3 (v9-13)		Sea, land and plants
Day 4 (v14-19)		Sun, moon and stars
Day 5 (v20-23)		Fish and birds
Day 6 (v24-31)		Animals and people

CREATION GAME
Children may like to make a simple game, using 12 pieces of card. On six cards <u>write</u> Day 1, Day 2...Day 6. On the other six <u>draw</u> what God made. The game is to to match what was made with the correct day. Children could use it to test visitors!

Do a quick whiz through **Genesis 1v3-25** to spot the words that keep popping up (v4,10,12,18,21, 25). When "God saw that it was good" it doesn't just mean that He liked it! The word "good" means that it was fit for the purpose God had made it for. Everything was just as God planned it.
None of it happened by accident!

DAY 18
Spot the difference

> **KEYPOINT**
> People are different from animals. We are made in God's image (likeness) and rule the rest of God's creation.

Today's passages are:
Table Talk: Genesis 1v26-28
XTB: Genesis 1v26-2v4

 TABLE TALK
Do you have any pets? How are you <u>different</u> from them? (e.g. you talk, draw...)

 **READ**
Yesterday we saw that God made *animals* on Day 6. Then He created *people*. **Read Genesis 1v26-28**

 **TALK**
Verse 26 tells us **two ways** that people are different from animals. What are they? (1—made in God's image, 2—rule over fish, birds and animals)

 **THINK**
People are made in God's likeness (image). That means made like God Himself! Wow! Does that mean we can do the amazing things God can do? (*No!*) But it <u>does</u> mean that human beings **rule** the rest of God's creation. (See v28) God has put us **in charge** of His world—to look after it and enjoy it.

(*Optional*) Read **Genesis 2v1-3** What did God do when He had finished creating the world? (*v2—He rested*) God wasn't tired! He stopped because He had **finished** His work, and it was exactly how He had planned it. Everything was perfect.

 PRAY
Thank God for creating a good world for us to live in. Ask Him to help you to look after it.

Building up
People sometimes say that we're no different from animals. How does **Genesis 1v26-27** help you answer that? Does this mean it doesn't matter how we treat animals? Why/why not?

DAY 19
Whose job is it anyway?

 > **KEYPOINT**
> It's <u>God's</u> job to decide what's good and bad—not ours.

Today's passages are:
Table Talk: Genesis 2v15-17
XTB: Genesis 2v4-17

 TABLE TALK
Test each other to see if you can remember what God made on each day. Check **Notes for Parents** on Day 17 if you're not sure.

 **READ**
Chapter Two of Genesis tells us more about the creation of man. Verse 7 says God made man "from the dust of the ground". Then God planted a garden for the man to live in.
Read Genesis 2v15-17

 **TALK**
What was the man to do? (v15) (*To work and take care of the garden*) God told the man he could eat from any tree except one. Which one? (v17) What would happen if he ate from it? (*He would die*)

 **THINK**
If the man eats from this tree, he will want to decide for himself what's good and bad. What's wrong with that? (*The world is* **God's** *place—He created it—He is King. It's* **God's job** *to decide what's good and what's bad.*)

 **PRAY**
Father God, thank you that You know the **best** way for us to live. You show us what's good and what's bad. Please help us to trust You and obey You.

Building up
The man had a **choice**—to obey God, or to eat from the forbidden tree. We have the **same choice**—to obey God or do what **we** want instead. Do you find it hard to believe that God always knows what's best? Why? (*Adults need to be honest here too.*) Ask God to help you to trust Him and to live His way.

DAY 20
She's the one!

> **KEYPOINT**
> It wasn't good for Adam to be alone, so God made Eve as a companion for Adam. She was like him, but different.

Today's passages are:
Table Talk: Genesis 2v18 + 20-23
XTB: Genesis 2v18-25

TABLE TALK

Name Game: Try to go right through the alphabet naming an animal for each letter. (e.g. Aardvark, Baboon, Camel...)

The first man—**Adam**—was living in a perfect garden, in a perfect world. But something wasn't good...
Read Genesis 2v18

READ

What **wasn't** good? (*Adam being alone*)

TALK

God brought the animals to Adam, so that he could name them all. But none of them could be Adam's companion, because people are **completely different** from animals (as we saw on Day 18). **Read Genesis 2v20-23**

What companion did God make for Adam? (*A woman*) What did God make her from? (*Adam's rib*) Do you know what Adam called his wife? (*Eve—Adam chooses this name in Genesis 3v20*)

The woman was just what Adam wanted. She was **like** him—but **different**. Thank God for creating both men and women, boys and girls.

PRAY

Building up
Did you know that marriage was invented by God? **Read Genesis 2v23-24** Adam's wife was very special to him because she came from his own body. God says all marriages are special—**two** people come together and form **one** partnership. Thank God for His great gift of marriage.

DAY 21
Snakes and ladders

> **KEYPOINT**
> Adam and Eve disobeyed God. They listened to the devil's lies, and ate the forbidden fruit.

Today's passages are:
Table Talk: Genesis 3v1-5
XTB: Genesis 3v1-7

TABLE TALK

(*You need paper & pencil*) Draw a picture to sum up what you know about Adam and Eve so far. (*e.g. garden, man and woman, trees, one tree they mustn't eat from...*)

READ

There was someone in the garden who wanted to spoil everything.
Read Genesis 3v1-5

TALK

What did the snake pretend that God had said? (*They mustn't eat from any tree in the garden*) Then the snake lied again. What did he say **wouldn't** happen? (v4) (*They wouldn't die*) What did he say **would** happen? (v5) (*They'd be like God, knowing what's good and bad*)

THINK

Whose job is it to decide what's good and bad? (**God's job**—*as we saw on Day 19*) But Eve listened to the snake's lies. She ate the fruit—and gave some to Adam too.

PRAY

The snake was the devil in disguise. The devil always wants us to disobey God. Ask God to help you **not to listen** to the devil's tempting ideas.

Building up
How would you explain **Sin** to someone? (*Discuss your ideas.*) This story helps us understand what sin is. Adam and Eve didn't want God to be King—to be in charge. They wanted to decide for themselves what was good and bad. They chose to do what **they** wanted instead of what **God** wanted. This is Sin.

DAY 22
Sin snapshots

KEYPOINT
Sin separates people from God. Adam and Eve had to leave the garden because of their sin.

Today's passages are:
Table Talk: Genesis 3v8-13
XTB: Genesis 3v8-24

TABLE TALK
Recap yesterday's story: What did the snake tell Eve? What did Adam & Eve do?

READ
Adam and Eve had disobeyed God. When they heard Him walking in the garden they hid. **Read Genesis 3v8-13**

TALK
God knew that Adam and Eve had eaten the forbidden fruit. Who did Adam blame? (v12) (*Eve*) Who did Eve blame? (v13) (*The snake*) Adam and Eve both <u>blamed</u> someone else—but they had both <u>chosen</u> to disobey God. They chose to sin. As a result (v23-24) they had to leave the perfect garden.

THINK
Sin **separates** people from God. Adam & Eve had to leave the garden because of their sin. They couldn't live with God for ever, as they were meant to. Sin gets in the way between **us** and God too. But who did God send to solve the problem of sin? (*JESUS—as we saw on Day 7*)

PRAY
Thank God for sending Jesus to solve the problem of sin.

Building up
Read God's curse on the snake (the devil) in **v14-15**. It sounds odd—but there's a great **promise** here. God is saying that one of Eve's family (her offspring) will <u>beat</u> the devil. Who is this about? (*This promise is all about Jesus—one of Eve's family—who came as our Rescuer to beat the problem of sin for ever.*) Thank God for keeping His promise to send Jesus.

DAY 23
Notes for Parents

Adam and Eve had two sons. Their eldest son, Cain, was a farmer. Their younger son was called Abel. He was a shepherd.

Cain and Abel both gave gifts to God. These were called offerings.

Cain gave God some of his crops.

Abel gave God the best of his flock.

God was pleased with Abel's gift. But He wasn't pleased with Cain's gift.

Cain was so angry that he took his brother Abel out to a field—and **killed** him!

DAY 23
The best way to live

KEYPOINT
Cain killed his brother Abel—the first murder. Cain's sin separated him from God.

Today's passages are:
Table Talk: Genesis 4v8-12
XTB: Genesis 4v1-16

Read the story of Cain and Abel in **Notes for Parents** (on the previous page).

Cain had just committed the first <u>murder</u>. Then God asked him where his brother was. **Read Genesis 4v8-12**

What did God ask Cain? (v9) What was Cain's answer? (v9) Cain lied, but <u>God knew</u> what he had done. How did God punish Cain? (v12) (*He wasn't able to grow crops any more. He became a wanderer, with no home.*)

See how sin **spreads**. Cain lied to God and murdered his brother. As a result of his sin he was **separated** from God (v16 makes this clear). Does this remind you of anything? (*e.g. Adam & Eve were separated from God because of their sin.*)

Say **sorry** to God for the times you disobey Him. **Thank** God that He's given us lots of help in the Bible to show us the <u>best way</u> to live.

Building up
It's tempting to think that being in charge of our own lives must be better than being told what to do. But this horrible story shows what happens when people live **without** God in charge. The Bible tells us that God always knows the **best** way for us to live. Do you believe that? Why/why not?

DAY 24
Build a lifeboat

KEYPOINT
People's hearts were so full of evil that God decided to flood the earth clean.

Today's passages are:
Table Talk: Genesis 6v5-8 + 22
XTB: Genesis 6v5-22

Find any Noah stuff you have. (*Books, toys, pictures, t-towels!!*) Use these to help you think about the story of Noah—but bear in mind that children's books may focus on cute animals rather than on God!

In the last two readings we've seen that **sin spreads**. Today we see just how far it had spread... **Read Genesis 6v5-8**

When God looked at the people, what did He see? (v5) (*Their hearts were full of evil*) How did God feel? (v6) (*Sorry that He had made them*) God was so sorry that He had made man, that He decided to flood the earth clean. But <u>one</u> man was different. Who? (Noah) What does verse 8 say about him?

God told Noah to build a boat (an ark) so that Noah and his family would be kept safe. (*The details are in v14-16*) Imagine being told to build a H-U-G-E boat—miles away from the sea! Would you do it? Why/why not? What would your friends say?

Read v22. Noah obeyed God <u>completely</u>. Do you want to be like Noah? Then ask God to help you.

Building up
Read **Genesis 1v31** and compare it with **Genesis 6v6**. What has changed between these two verses? Why?

DAY 25
Into the ark

KEYPOINT
Noah obeyed God completely. He built the ark, filled it with food, and pairs of every animal and bird.

Today's passages are:
Table Talk: Genesis 7v1-5
XTB: Genesis 7v1-10

 TABLE TALK
How many birds can you name in one minute?

 **READ**
Noah had built the ark, and filled it with food for all. Now it was time to get on board. **Read Genesis 7v1-5**

 **TALK**
How many <u>animals</u> did Noah take? *(7 pairs of each clean animal, 2 pairs of each unclean animal—see **Building Up** below if you want more information.)* How many pairs of <u>birds</u> did Noah take? *(7 of each kind)* It would start raining in seven days time. How long would it rain for? (v4) *(40 days and 40 nights)* What does v5 tell you about Noah? *(He obeyed God totally)*

Have you ever tried to catch a pet that doesn't want to be caught? Noah couldn't possibly catch all those animals and birds! So God made them **come** to Noah! (*"they will come to you"* 6v20, *"they came to Noah and entered the ark"* 7v9 NIV)

Noah <u>obeyed</u> God by doing what he could do—and <u>trusted</u> God to look after the rest. Ask God to help you to do the same.

PRAY

Building up
Whether an animal was **clean** or **unclean** had nothing to do with mud! The clean animals (like sheep) were the ones that could be offered to God as a gift (a sacrifice). Any animal offered to God had to be **perfect**. Thousands of years later, the death of Jesus was the ultimate, perfect sacrifice to God.
See 1 Peter 1v18-19

DAY 26
God's great rescue

KEYPOINT
Sin must be punished, but God provides a way to be rescued.

Today's passages are:
Table Talk: Genesis 7v20-24
XTB: Genesis 7v11-24

 TABLE TALK
Find a very simple jigsaw. (About 20 pieces.) Time how long it takes you to do it.

 **READ**
The Bible fits together like a Giant Jigsaw. All the way through we find the <u>same</u> <u>two</u> things. **1—Sin must be punished**. **2—God provides a way to be rescued**. Look out for these two things in the story of Noah.

The flood waters kept coming for 40 days. Everything was under water—even the highest mountains!
Read Genesis 7v20-24

 **TALK**
1—Sin must be punished. At the beginning of chapter 6 we saw how wicked the people had become (6v5). How did God punish them? *(The flood)* **2—God provides a rescue.** God provided a way to be rescued from the flood. What was it? *(The ark)* Who was rescued? (v23)

 PRAY
The Bible says that Jesus is the greatest Rescuer of all. (Matthew 1v21) <u>Everyone</u> sins. We **all** disobey God and deserve to be punished. Thank God for sending Jesus to be your Rescuer.

Building up
<u>Why</u> were Noah and his family rescued? (See Genesis 7v1) <u>Note</u>: This doesn't mean that Noah was perfect! Who is the only perfect man to have lived? *(Jesus)* But Noah did obey God—and he trusted God to rescue him.

DAY 27 God remembers Noah

KEYPOINT
God kept His promise to rescue Noah and his family. He sent a wind to dry up the flood waters.

Today's passages are:
Table Talk: Genesis 8v6-12
XTB: Genesis 8v1-14

 TABLE TALK
How do you remember things? (*a diary? a knot in your handkerchief? an alarm?...*)

Genesis 8v1 says "God <u>remembered</u> Noah". God doesn't forget things!! When God **remembered** Noah it means He **acted** on His promise to rescue Noah from the flood. He sent a wind to dry up the water.

The flood waters were going down. Now Noah had to find a way to check if the floods had completely gone.
 **READ**
Read Genesis 8v6-12

 **TALK**
What two birds did Noah send out? (*A raven & a dove*) What happened the first time he sent the dove? (v9) (*It came back with nothing*) The second time? (v11) (*It brought back an olive leaf—so Noah knew the water had gone*) The third time? (v12) (*It didn't come back*)

 PRAY
God remembered Noah and his family. He had promised to keep them safe—and He did. Thank God for always keeping His promises.

Building up
Read **Genesis 7v11 & 8v13-14** to work out how long Noah and his family lived on the ark. (*Just over a year!*) Imagine spending a year on a boat with all those animals! The noise! The smell! Do you think Noah found it easy? Why do you think he kept trusting God all that time? Ask God to help you to trust Him patiently as Noah did.

DAY 28 Out of the ark

KEYPOINT
Noah thanked God for rescuing him. God promised never again to destroy all living things.

Today's passages are:
Table Talk: Genesis 8v20-22
XTB: Genesis 8v15-22

 TABLE TALK
Try to mimic the sounds Noah had been listening to for a year. (*e.g. water slapping the ark, the wood creaking, animal noises, bird calls...*)

God told Noah and his family to come out of the ark—so they did. After leaving the ark, Noah gave thanks to God. He took some of the "clean" animals and offered them to God as a gift.
 **READ**
Read Genesis 8v20-22

TALK
God was pleased with Noah's offering and thankfulness. What did God promise? (v21) (*Never again to destroy all living things*) Instead, God promised that for as long as the earth exists some things will <u>never end</u>. What are they? (v22) (*e.g. cold & heat, day & night...*)

 **PRAY**
Look again at the list in v22, Which of these is true for **you** right now? Thank God that these things remind you that God is keeping His promise to take care of our world.

Building up
Read **Genesis 6v14**
Who told Noah to build the ark?
Read **7v1** Who told Noah to enter the ark?
Read **7v16** Who closed the door of the ark?
Read **8v15-16** Who told Noah to come out of the ark? What do these verses tell you about God? (*e.g. He's in control of every detail, He keeps His promises, He's a God who rescues...*)

DAY 29
Rainbow promises

KEYPOINT
God made a covenant (a binding agreement) with Noah—never again to destroy the earth.

Today's passages are:
Table Talk: Genesis 9v8-13
XTB: Genesis 9v1-17

TABLE TALK

Rainbow Fun: Do you know the colours of the rainbow? (*Red, Orange, Yellow, Green, Blue, Indigo, Violet*) A traditional (if rather boring!) way to remember them is "**R**ichard **O**f **Y**ork **G**ave **B**attle **I**n **V**ain". Can you make up a better one instead?

READ

Now that the floods had gone down, God made a **covenant** (a binding agreement) with Noah and his family.
Read Genesis 9v8-13

TALK

Who did God make His covenant with? (v9-10) (*Noah, his family [descendants] and every living creature*) What did God promise? (v11) (*Never again to destroy the earth*) What is the sign of God's covenant? (*The rainbow*)

DO

(*Optional*) Draw a rainbow. Write **"God always keeps His promises"** under it. Stick it on your wall—or send it to someone else to remind them of God's faithfulness.

PRAY

Thank God for keeping the promise He made to Noah, to all of creation and to <u>you</u>.

Building up
The account of Noah shows us God's character. **Psalm 145** praises God for who He is. If you have time, read the whole Psalm. Otherwise, just read **v8-13** which praise God for His compassion towards His creation. Thank God for being like this.

DAY 30
A perfect man?

KEYPOINT
The NT sums up Noah. He wasn't perfect—only Jesus is!—but he trusted and obeyed God.

Today's passages are:
Table Talk: Hebrews 11v7
XTB: Hebrews 11v7

TABLE TALK

Briefly retell the whole story of Noah, using Noah pictures or toys if you have any. Choose <u>two</u> words that describe what Noah was like.

READ

Find out what one part of the New Testament says about Noah…
Read Hebrews 11v7

TALK

What <u>two key things</u> does the book of Hebrews tell us about Noah? (*He had **faith** in God. He **obeyed** God.*)

THINK

Noah stood out among the other people of his time. He was the <u>only</u> one who trusted and obeyed God. Does his story help **you** to trust and obey God? Why? (*e.g. we've seen that God always keeps His promises*)

PRAY

Dear God, Thank you that You always keep Your promises. Please help us to **trust** You. Thank you that You show us the best way to live. Please help us to **obey** You. Amen

Building up
Genesis 9 ends with an odd little story, where Noah planted the first vineyard, turned the grapes into wine—and got drunk! Then his son Ham didn't treat Noah with the respect he should have shown. (Genesis 9v18-29) Noah and his family were <u>not</u> perfect! (*There is only one perfect man—**Jesus**.*) But we can still learn loads from Noah's faith and obedience. Thank God for the things you've learnt from Noah's life.

DAYS 31-50
Notes for Parents

MATTHEW'S GOSPEL
The next 20 days are based in Matthew's Gospel. (*Gospel* means *Good News*.) The first four chapters cover the birth of Jesus and His early ministry. Then we will be investigating part of a big block of teaching called The Sermon on the Mount (*chapters 5-7*).

As we'll see, Matthew squeezed in loads of chunks from the Old Testament. He did this because the Old T is full of promises about a new king...

God's Promise to Abraham

God promised that one of Abraham's family would be God's way of **blessing** the whole world. *(Genesis 12v3 + 22v18)*

God's Promise to David

God promised that one of David's family would be a **King** who would rule for ever and ever. *(2 Samuel 7v12 + 16)*

God's Promise to His People

God promised that He would send a **rescuer**, called the Messiah or Christ. *(e.g. Isaiah 53v4-6, Zechariah 9v9)*

DAY 31
Family tree

KEYPOINT
Matthew starts with Jesus' family tree, to show He is the King promised to Abraham and David.

Today's passages are:
Table Talk: Matthew 1v1
XTB: Matthew 1v1-17

 TABLE TALK
Talk about your family. Who is in your family? Who is your mum's mum? Who is your dad's sister? and so on.

 **DO**
(*Optional*) Work together to draw your own family tree. This can be quick, if just close family, or the start of a longer term project.

 **READ**
Matthew's book starts with a family tree.
Read Matthew 1v1

 **TALK**
A "genealogy" (NIV) lists a person's family line. Which three people are listed in verse 1? (*Jesus, David, Abraham*) God promised Abraham and David that someone from their family would be a great King. Who do you think this King was? (*JESUS. The title Christ means "God's chosen King"*)

(Optional) Read **Notes for Parents** opposite for more details of God's promises.

 **PRAY**
Jesus had a human family like we do. Thank God for your family and pray for each person in it.

Building up
Why did Matthew want us to know that Jesus comes from the same family as Abraham and David? (*To show that God kept His promise to Abraham and David to send Jesus as the King*) Does it <u>matter</u> that God keeps His promises? Why?

DAY 32
A King is born

KEYPOINT
The name Jesus means "God Saves". It tells us who He is (God) and what He does (He saves).

Today's passages are:
Table Talk: Matthew 1v21
XTB: Matthew 1v18-25

 **TABLE TALK** Talk about your names. <u>Who</u> chose each person's name? <u>Why</u> did they choose that name? Were you nearly called something else instead?

 **READ** Before the birth of Jesus, God sent an angel as His messenger to Joseph. Read part of the angel's message in **Matthew 1v21**

 **TALK** Who chose the name Jesus? (*God did—the angel gave <u>God's</u> message*) In Bible times names were often chosen because of their meaning. The name Jesus means "God saves". Why is this a good name for Him? (*Because His name helps us to remember who Jesus is [God] and what He does [He saves us from our sins].*)

 **DO** (*Optional*) Write the words **"Jesus—God Saves"** on a large sheet of paper. Stick it on the wall as a reminder.

 PRAY Thank God for sending Jesus to save us.

Building up
Read Matthew 1v18-25 Verse 23 gives another name for Jesus. What is it, and what does it mean? (*Immanuel—God with us*) What does it mean that Jesus is "God with us" today?

DAY 33
Growing all the time

KEYPOINT
Wise men travelled from the East to see the young Jesus—the promised King.

Today's passages are:
Table Talk: Matthew 2v9-11
XTB: Matthew 2v1-12

 TABLE TALK Talk about some recent visitors to your home (or due soon). Why did they come? Who are your favourite visitors and why?

 **READ** After Jesus was born, wise men (Magi) travelled from the East to see Him. Their long journey ended in Bethlehem.
Read Matthew 2v9-11

 **TALK** Who came to visit the young Jesus? (*Children will probably include the shepherds as well as the wise men.*) What presents did the wise men give? (v11) (*Note: Frankincense smells sweet when burnt. Myrrh was used as a spice and a medicine.*)

 **THINK** The wise men came a huge distance to see Jesus. Why do you think they did that? When they found Jesus they gave Him presents and worshipped Him. What could <u>you</u> do today to show that you love Jesus?

 **PRAY** Ask God to help you to show your love for Jesus.

Building up
Before reaching Bethlehem, the wise men had a meeting with evil King Herod. Herod didn't want anyone else to be king—but he pretended that he did. **Read Matthew 2v8** The wise men <u>really</u> worshipped Jesus. King Herod only <u>pretended</u>. Do **you** really worship Jesus? Or are you just pretending? What can you do to show that you love Jesus and believe He is the King?

HELP! Is my child a Christian?

I know that you don't want to hear this, but let me say it anyway. **There is no set formula that will guarantee that your child grows up Christian.** Salvation is God's work, not ours. His Spirit blows where He wills. We all long for our kids to be committed Christians, and will work and pray fervently to that end. But, under God, it may not happen! That does not mean we have 'failed' as parents. There are many wonderful Christian parents who have faithfully modelled godly Christian living and brought up their children to know and love the Lord Jesus and have yet to see any fruit from their labours.

We need to relax and trust God. Our job is to be faithful to our calling to love and teach those in our care. Just as children are a gift from God for which we should be thankful, so the kids we have been given, with their individual personalities, strengths, faults and sinful hearts, have been given to us by God. We must accept what God has given and with Him work to shape them into responsible and mature adults who will hopefully embrace the gospel and love Jesus as their Lord.

It can, however, be a nerve-wracking experience. Children go through many phases as they grow. There may be times when they love going to church, are keen on reading the Bible, and pray prayers that leave you tearful with their sincerity and simple trust. There will be other times when they are bored with the whole thing, resistant to reading with you, and prone to giggle or play around when you make the mistake of closing your eyes to pray!

There are a variety of views among Christians about how we treat our children. Some people falsely believe that if you have your child baptised or 'Christened' that it makes them a member of the kingdom of God. This is clearly wrong—getting wet has never been a means of forgiveness.

The marks of someone who truly belongs to Christ are easier to spot in adults: eg A love for the Word of God; a desire to please God and compassion for others. But spotting the marks of genuine belief in children is much harder, if not impossible.

Christian parents generally take one of two views:

1. We should treat our children as <u>not</u> being Christian until they opt in.

2. We should treat our children as Christian until they opt out.

But whichever view you take makes little difference to the practicalities of what you actually *do* with them. Whether you view them as little pagans or baby Christians, you still do the same thing: **you teach them the Word of God.** That is, you open up the Bible's message about who God is, and what He has done for us in Christ.

The Bible is God speaking to us. And what He tells us will have the effect of bringing us to salvation through Jesus' death and resurrection, and enabling us to grow as His disciples. So whichever state you believe your child to be in, what they need is to hear God's word explained to them clearly, and to receive the challenge it gives to believe in Him and to follow His ways.

Even so, it can be worrying to feel that your child is slipping away from Christian things. Here are some pointers if you are concerned about this:

1. DON'T PANIC

God is sovereign—He's in control. You may be desperate for your child to come to an assured faith, but remember that this is not in your gift. Only God can give faith and eternal life.

2. BE PATIENT

A time of disinterest in Christian things is common–for some it lasts longer than others. It's easy for you to get annoyed, frustrated or even angry that your children don't seem to be responding to the Gospel. Take the long view. As in any kind of evangelism, pressurising people is nearly always counter-productive.

3. MODEL GENUINE DISCIPLESHIP

Show how important following Christ is to you. Try to read the Bible and pray yourself at a time when they can see or listen in. They will catch more from your own seriousness and enthusiasm than they will by hearing you tell them to do it a hundred times over. And try to be honest about your own struggles. Ask your children to pray for you when you are worried or upset about things. Admit that you find certain of God's ways puzzling, while showing how you trust Him for the things that you do not understand. And talk to them about what you have learned from your own Bible reading. When you do this, you show them that you are not a 'know it all', but rather a disciple—someone who is learning about Jesus day by day.

4. KEEP PRAYING

God is sovereign—He's in control, and He longs to answer our prayers. Although there are still no promises, it is the testimony of many praying parents that, even after long years in the wilderness, their errant children have returned to the fold.

5. KEEP SOWING THE SEED

It may be that you need to change how you do things, but continue to sow the seed of the Word. What works well with infants will need to change again at primary school, and again as your children progress. It may be that they tire of a routine that has worked well for a long time. A shift from bedtime reading to the early morning, or the dinner table may be required. You might change the style of your Bible time to a question and answer session, or to dramatically re-enacting Bible stories.

And our teaching of God's word should not be confined to a set Bible time. It is important that children should see that talking about the Lord is as natural as any other conversation: 'When you sit at home and when you walk along the road, when you lie down and when you get up.' (Deut 6: 4-9). So the sight of a rainbow should never pass without you reminding them of God's judgement and His promises. A nature walk should never stop at a scientific explanation, but always wonder at the greatness, beauty and humour of the Lord our creator. And likewise, news stories, or bad news in the family needs to be kept in the context of the sinfulness of mankind and God's ultimate purposes for the world if our children are to grow up with a Christian understanding.

> *Whether you view them as little pagans or as baby Christians, you still do the same thing: you teach them the Word of God*

Is your child a Christian? It's very difficult to tell for sure. But whatever the truth, our role as parents remains the same: to ensure that our children's grasp of the knowledge of God grows in step as they mature both physically and mentally.

Just as we feed them with nutritious food, appealingly presented; and just as we introduce their growing minds to new ideas and books as they get older; so too we must strive to serve up the milk and then the meat of God's word in an appealing and appropriate manner.

It is our prayer that **Table Talk** and **XTB** will inspire and help you as you seek to be faithful to the God who saved you and who entrusted you with your child.

Tim Thornborough
Father of three...

DAY 34
Notes for Parents

WHY DOES GOD...?
The reading for Day 34 includes Herod's plans to murder the young Jesus. For some children, particularly older ones, this may be a good time to discuss why God allows such things to happen:

Focus on a current or recent news item such as a war, terrorist attack or man-made disaster. Talk with your child about their feelings when such things happen. Explain that events like these are often caused by people who <u>don't care</u> about God or His laws. For example, wars can often be traced back to greed, pride or hatred.

Read Matthew 2v13-18

The dreadful murders in today's passage happened because Herod was jealous and angry at the idea of anyone else being king. But Matthew shows clearly that God was <u>always</u> in control. Herod was unable to stop God's plans—in fact he ended up fulfilling them instead!

It can be very hard to understand why God lets these bad things happen, but the Bible tells us that God is always in control. Pray about this—asking God to help you to trust Him, even when it's hard to do so.

PLEASE NOTE
A Table Talk suggestions for Day 34 (suitable for younger children) can be found opposite.

DAY 34
Escape to Egypt

KEYPOINT
Herod wanted to stop God's plans, but he couldn't. God was always in control.

Today's passages are:
Table Talk: Matthew 2v13-15
XTB: Matthew 2v12-23

 TABLE TALK

*Note: Today's section is designed particularly with <u>younger</u> children in mind. Suggestions for older children can be found in **Notes for Parents** opposite.*

Talk about people who have moved away to live somewhere else. Why do people move? (*Ask for both happy & sad reasons.*)

 **READ**

Evil King Herod didn't want anyone else to be king. He planned to kill Jesus—so God sent an angel to warn Joseph to escape to Egypt.
Read Matthew 2v13-15

 **TALK**

Who told Joseph to take Mary and Jesus to Egypt? (*An angel—giving God's message*) They left in the middle of the night (v14). Why did they need to leave so quickly? (*To escape from Herod*) Who kept Jesus safe from King Herod? (*God did*) Point out that Jesus was <u>always</u> safe, because God was <u>always</u> in control.

 **PRAY**

God is always in control, even when things are difficult or frightening. Ask God to help you to trust Him, even when it is hard.

Building up
Today's Table Talk notes show that God is in control, even when Herod tries to kill Jesus.

Please see **Notes for Parents** on the previous page for suggestions for how to build on today's Table Talk and XTB notes.

DAY 35
Locusts for lunch

> **KEYPOINT**
> John the Baptist was God's messenger, sent to tell people to get ready for King Jesus.

Today's passages are:
Table Talk: Matthew 3v1-4
XTB: Matthew 3v1-6

TABLE TALK

Together, invent some wacky suggestions for a meal. (*Custard on cornflakes, jam on sausages, peas with honey?*) Maybe you could try some out at your next meal time!

READ

By the time we reach chapter three of Matthew, Jesus is grown up. So is His cousin John the Baptist.
Read Matthew 3v1-4

TALK

What did John the Baptist eat and wear? (v4)

(*Optional*) Look up **2 Kings 1v8** to see which Old Testament prophet this reminded people of. (*Elijah*)

Old Testament prophets were God's messengers. John the Baptist was a messenger too. He told people about **Jesus**. How can *we* learn more about Jesus? (*e.g. the Bible, church, other Christians...*) Who can help us?

PRAY

Pray for people who tell you (and others) about Jesus.

Building up
Matthew 3 introduces John the Baptist as God's promised messenger—telling people to repent (turn away from their sin) and get ready for King Jesus.
Read Matthew 3v5-6
John baptised people in the river Jordan. It showed that they wanted to be washed clean from their sins, ready to welcome King Jesus. What kind of things <u>stop</u> people from welcoming Jesus? Do any of these stop <u>you</u>? Pray about your answer.

DAY 36
Notes for Parents

SIN AND REPENTANCE
The reading for Day 36 introduces the themes of sin and repentance.

Children often think of **sin** as doing wrong things (especially "BIG" things like stealing or killing). However, the Bible view of sin is much wider (and deeper) than this.

One helpful way to explain it is to use the idea of **kingship**. God is our **King**. He created us and rules over us. But we all reject God. We  want to be in charge of our own lives, rather than letting God be our ruler. This rejection of God's rule over us is what the Bible means by sin.

> **Repent** is another word that may need explaining. It means more than just saying sorry. It means asking God to help us to <u>change</u>, to stop living for ourselves (as king of our own life) and to live the way God our King wants us to live instead.

Many children are all too familiar with disobedience! They get into trouble at home and school, or see others who do. However, it can be very helpful to them to know that <u>adults</u> also find it hard to obey God.

This is a good opportunity to be honest with one another, adults and children together, and accountable to each other. Parents can help children to obey God—and children can also help parents!

One word of caution. Talk of 'good behaviour' will reinforce many children's impression that the Gospel is all about Works (what we do). Make sure Grace (God's free gift) is the main theme!

DAY 36
Rotten apples?

KEYPOINT
John told people they needed to repent (turn away from sin), and live for God from now on.

Today's passages are:
Table Talk: Matthew 3v8
XTB: Matthew 3v7-12

 Talk about times when it is difficult to obey God. (*It is important that adults are honest about this too, so that children see that we all struggle with obedience at times.*) Why do we find it hard?

 When people don't care about obeying God, you can see it in the way they live. They're like fruit trees that don't grow fruit! Read the passage to see what John says they should do.
Read Matthew 3v8

 John said that we're to be like fruit trees that grow **good fruit**, showing that we have **repented** (turned away from our sins). Think of some examples. (e.g. *Instead of being selfish, we should... Instead of lying to get out of trouble, we should...*)

 To repent doesn't just mean saying sorry. It also means changing—to turn away from sin and live the way God wants us to. Pray about this together, telling God you are sorry for disobeying Him and asking Him to help you to change.

Building up
Please see **Notes for Parents** on the previous page for suggestions how to build on today's Table Talk and XTB notes. Be ready to be honest with your child about your own need to repent.

DAY 37
The King is baptised

KEYPOINT
Jesus was baptised. The Spirit came down like a dove, and God called Jesus His loved Son

Today's passages are:
Table Talk: Matthew 3v16-17
XTB: Matthew 3v13-17

 Discuss any experience of baptism your child has had or seen. If they have been baptised themselves, talk about what happened and why. Photos might help. If you are waiting for them to make their own decision about baptism when older, then talk about why this is. If your church practises adult baptism, talk about a recent example.

 Jesus was baptised by John in the river Jordan. **Read Matthew 3v16-17**

 What happened when Jesus came out of the water? (*The Spirit came down like a dove and God spoke*) What did God say about Jesus? (*Jesus is His Son, He loves Jesus, He is pleased with Jesus*)

 Pray for anyone you know who has just been or soon will be baptised.

Building up
Is baptism the same as having a bath? *Why/why not?*

Being **baptised** is like being washed clean on the <u>outside</u>. Being **forgiven** is like being washed clean on the <u>inside</u>. Baptism is an <u>outside</u> sign of an <u>inside</u> change.

Anyone can take a bath, but only **one person** can wash us clean on the inside. Who?

DAY 38
Tempting times

KEYPOINT
The devil tempted Jesus to do wrong—but Jesus never sinned. God promises to help us when we are tempted.

Today's passages are:
Table Talk: Matthew 4v1
XTB: Matthew 4v1-11

TABLE TALK
Which of these have you ever been tempted to do?—lying, gossiping, swearing, being greedy, fighting. (*It's important that everyone is honest here, adults as well as children.*)

READ
Jesus knows what it is like to be tempted. **Read Matthew 4v1** (*If you have older children, and enough time, then read the full passage, v1-11.*)

TALK
Who tempted Jesus to do wrong? (*The devil*) The devil is sometimes called the tempter. He tempts us to do things which displease God—and he is delighted when we give in.

(Optional) Look up **1 Corinthians 10v13** together.

THINK
In 1 Cor 10v13 God promises to give us a way out when tempted. How do you think God might do that?

Pray about this together, asking God to help you when you're tempted to do wrong.

PRAY

Building up
The full passage shows Jesus' response to the devil's tempting. **Read Matthew 4v1-11**

Jesus gives an example for us to follow. What can we do when tempted? Pray about this together.

DAY 39
King's kingdom

KEYPOINT
Jesus travelled all over Israel preaching—telling people how they can be right with God.

Today's passages are:
Table Talk: Matthew 4v17
XTB: Matthew 12v17

TABLE TALK
(*You need a local map.*) Find your home or street on a map. Can you find any other places on the map that you have walked to? What is the farthest you have walked? Why did you walk there?

READ
In Matthew chapter 4, Jesus begins to travel around the country of Israel. He probably walked between towns. Read the passage to find out why He travelled so far. **Read Matthew 4v17**
(*See Notes for Parents on Day 36 for an explanation of the word "repent".*)

TALK
Jesus travelled all over the country because He had something very important to do. What was it? (*To preach—to tell people how they can be right with God and live with Him in charge, as their King.*) Why was it important for Jesus to preach to people?

PRAY
Pray for someone you know who travels to tell people about Jesus.

Building up
Read Matthew 4v12-17

Jesus preached **"Repent, for the kingdom of heaven is near."** (v17) What do you think this means? How would you explain it to a friend? (*The kingdom of heaven was near because Jesus the King had arrived. People needed to repent, and follow Him as King of their lives.*)

DAY 40
Follow me

KEYPOINT
Jesus called Peter and Andrew to follow Him. They were to tell other people about Jesus too.

Today's passages are:
Table Talk: Matthew 4v18-20
XTB: Matthew 4v18-25

 TABLE TALK
How many of Jesus' disciples can you remember between you? Check your answers in Matthew 10v2-4.

 **READ**
Read Matthew 4v18-20 to see how two men became disciples.

 **TALK**
Which two men did Jesus call to follow Him? (*Peter [Simon] and Andrew*) What were they doing when Jesus spoke to them? (*Fishing*) What new job did Jesus give them? (*To catch men!*)

 **DO**
(Optional) Ask your child to creep up behind you and pretend to catch you in a net!

Peter & Andrew weren't going to catch people in nets! What does "fisher of men" mean? (*To tell people about Jesus, so they can follow Him too.*) Who tells people about Jesus today? (*All Christians.*)

 PRAY
Ask God to help you to tell other people all about Jesus.

Building up
Read about two more fishermen in **Matthew 4v21-22** Notice how all four men left everything to follow Jesus. Do <u>we</u> have to leave our homes to follow Jesus? (*No!*) What do you think it means to be a follower of Jesus today? Are <u>you</u> following Jesus? (*If you're not sure, who could help you to find out?*)

DAY 41-50
Notes for Parents

THE SERMON ON THE MOUNT
Chapters 5-7 of Matthew contain a large block of Jesus' teaching called **The Sermon on the Mount** (because Jesus was on a mountain at the time). Jesus was teaching His **disciples** (Mt 5v1), although the crowds were there too, listening in (7v28).

BEING DIFFERENT
In Matthew 6v8 Jesus says, "**Do not be like them**". This verse sums up the flavour of the Sermon on the Mount. This <u>isn't</u> general moral guidance for good living. Jesus is teaching His <u>followers</u>. He is showing them how to live as subjects in the Kingdom of God. They are to be **different** from those around them. They are to be committed to living for their King.

DIPPING IN
Table Talk is just dipping in to parts of the Sermon on the Mount, to get the flavour of Jesus' teaching here. If your children are old enough to cope with longer readings, you will find it helpful to read the full **XTB** passage each day, rather than just the shorter verses suggested in Table Talk. You may also want to read other parts of the sermon, which are not covered in the notes.

Note: Much of the teaching in this sermon is about good living. Please make sure that your children are clear that they don't <u>become</u> part of God's Kingdom by keeping His rules. It is <u>because</u> we have been rescued by the King, that we want to live for Him— not the other way round!

DAY 41
The King teaches

> **KEYPOINT**
> Jesus starts the Sermon on the Mount by teaching that the Kingdom of God belongs to those who are spiritually poor.

Today's passages are:
Table Talk: Matthew 5v1-3
XTB: Matthew 5v1-5

Have you ever climbed a hill? What did you do at the top?(*A picnic? Take photos?*)

Jesus and His disciples went up a hill—but not to take photos! Jesus had some important teaching to do...

Read Matthew 5v1-3

This block of teaching is called The Sermon on the Mount. Why? (v1) Who is Jesus teaching? (v1) (*His disciples—those who are following Him*) Who does Jesus say the kingdom of heaven belongs to? (v3) (*The spiritually poor*)

What do you think it means to be spiritually poor? (*To know that you have nothing to offer God—that you're totally dependent on His kindness [grace]*) You can't <u>earn</u> your place in God's kingdom by being good! Why is that great news? (*Because none of us can be totally good all the time!*)

Forgiveness of sins, and a place in God's kingdom, is a <u>free gift</u>. Thank God for it.

Building up
Verses 3-12 are called the Beatitudes. Some people call them the "how-to-be attitudes". **Read v3-5** These verses apply to our attitude to God. People who please God **mourn**—they are sad because they know they disobey God. People who please God are **humble**—they look at how great <u>God</u> is, rather than being proud of how good <u>they</u> are. Are these <u>your</u> attitudes? Do you want them to be? If so, ask God to help you.

DAY 42
What are you doing?

> **KEYPOINT**
> People who follow Jesus hunger to do what He wants them to do

Today's passages are:
Table Talk: Matthew 5v6
XTB: Matthew 5v6-12

Imagine doing a survey outside a supermarket, asking people "What do you <u>most</u> want in life?" What do you think they will say? (e.g. money, family, new car...)

In v6 people want something <u>so much</u> it's as if they're really **hungry** for it! But it's not food... **Read Matthew 5v6**

What the person who follows Jesus wants <u>most</u> is to do is what <u>God</u> wants him to do. (To live in a **right** way before God). Will God give them what they want? (*Yes!—their "hunger" will be filled/satisfied*)

(*Optional*) **Read v7-9** to see what else Jesus' followers will be like.

Do you "hunger" to do what God wants you to do? If you do, that's great! But you can't do it on your own! Ask God to help you.

Father God, help us to do what You want us to do, and not to give up when we find it hard. Amen

Building up
Read Matthew 5v10-12 Will following Jesus be easy? (*No!*) You may get laughed at, or even lose some friends. What will you do if that happens? Will you give up? What does v12 say you should do? (*Rejoice!!*) Why should you be happy? (*Because you follow Jesus as your King <u>now</u>, v10, and will <u>one day</u> be with Him in heaven, v12*)

DAY 43
Make a difference

KEYPOINT
People who follow Jesus make a BIG difference to the world. They are like salt and light.

Today's passages are:
Table Talk: Matthew 5v13-16
XTB: Matthew 5v13-16

TABLE TALK
(You need a candle, and salt.) Light a **candle**. What does the flame look like? What <u>difference</u> does light make? Pour some **salt** into a saucer. Each person taste it. What does it taste like? What <u>difference</u> does salt make? (e.g. in cooking, on fish & chips...)

READ
People who follow Jesus make a BIG difference to the world. Jesus described them as <u>salt</u> and <u>light</u>.
Read Matthew 5v13-16

TALK
Why don't we put a candle under a bowl? (*The light would be hidden*) What does Jesus say His followers should do? (*Let their light shine before others*)

Jesus explains in v16 how to let our light shine. What should we do? (*Live the way God wants us to live*) What will happen when we do this? (*People will praise God—our Father in heaven*)

PRAY
Living the way God wants us to will make a BIG difference to the world. Ask God to help you to do this—so that people will find out about God and praise Him.

Building up
Read Matthew 5v13 Today we often use salt to add **flavour**—but in the ancient world it was also used to **preserve** food, and keep it fresh without a fridge. Our world is like meat that is rotting and going off! How? (*Because it doesn't obey God.*) How we can be like <u>salt</u> to the world? (*By showing a rotting world how God <u>does</u> want us to live.*)

DAY 44
Secret not showy

KEYPOINT
Jesus taught that His followers should give generously—but secretly.

Today's passages are:
Table Talk: Matthew 6v3-4
XTB: Matthew 6v1-4

TABLE TALK
Each find one thing that was given to you as a present. **Who** gave it to you? **Why**? (e.g. a birthday present, a thank you gift, just because they love you...)

READ
Some religious leaders liked to give gifts to the poor—but they made sure other people saw them do it! Jesus told His followers not to be like that!
Read Matthew 6v3-4

TALK
How does Jesus say <u>we</u> should give? (*In secret—privately*) Who <u>will</u> see what we do? (v4) (*God will!*)

THINK
Think of someone you could give help to this week. (*It may be a toy for a child who doesn't have many, a cooked meal for someone who's sick, weeding the garden for an elderly neighbour, or giving money to a charity.*) Now do it—and don't tell anyone!!

PRAY
Ask God to help you to be generous to others—and to help you to do it without boasting.

Building up
Read Matthew 6v1-2 The word "hypocrite" literally means "actor" i.e. they were just pretending! Why did they choose this way to give? (v2) (*So that other people would praise them.*) How can you make sure that you do things just to please <u>God</u>—not to impress other people? (*One way is to keep it all secret.*)

DAY 45 Please God —not people

KEYPOINT
Our prayers should be to please God, not to impress other people

Today's passages are:
Table Talk: Matthew 6v5-6
XTB: Matthew 6v5-8

 Where have you prayed in the last week? (*e.g. your bedroom, at church, wherever you do Table Talk...*) Any unusual places? (*In the bath? On a bike? Up a tree?*)

 The religious leaders prayed in places where everyone would see them—like street corners!
Read Matthew 6v5-6

 Where did the hypocrites ("actors") pray? (*Synagogues and street corners*) Where does Jesus say we should pray? (*In our room, in private*) Who will see us? (*God will*)

Does Jesus mean we can only pray in our rooms? (*No! We can pray anywhere and at any time*) So why does Jesus say to pray in our room? (*It's a good place because we're not worrying what other people think of us*)

PRAY It's great that we can pray anywhere and any time—but it's also good to set aside a specific time and place to pray, when nothing and nobody will disturb you. What would be a good time and place for each of you? Set a time and place—and ask God to help you to keep it.

Building up
Read v7-8 The pagans (non-believers) didn't know what God was like. How did they think they needed to pray? (*Using loads of long words.*) We don't need to repeat things loads of times, or to use lots of long words when we pray. Give thanks to God that He's not like this!

DAY 46 Long words or large prayers?

KEYPOINT
Jesus taught His followers The Lord's Prayer as a model of how to pray—God first, Us second.

Today's passages are:
Table Talk: Matthew 6v9-13
XTB: Matthew 6v7-15

 Imagine a young child asking you how to pray. What would you tell them?

 Jesus was teaching His followers about prayer. He'd told them how not to pray—not in public, not boastfully, or with loads of long words. Now He gave them an example of how to pray.
Read Matthew 6v9-13

 Do you know what this prayer is called? (*The Lord's Prayer*) The first part is all about **GOD**. Spot which verse matches each of these points.

A: Tell God how holy and amazing He is. (*Answer—v9*)
B: Ask for people to be saved into God's kingdom. (*v10*)
C: Ask for God's will to be done, not ours. (*v10*)

The second part is about **US**. Again find the verses to match each point.
D: Ask for what you really need. (*v11*)
E: Ask God to forgive you for the wrongs you've done. (*v12*)
F: Ask God to help you not to do wrong. (*v13*)

 Read v9-13 aloud as a prayer.

Building up
Verse 11 says "Give us today our daily bread." (NIV) Why don't we pray, "Give us today a year's supply of cream cakes"?! (*We're praying for what we need, not what we want, and just for one day at a time.*) Does God know what we need? (*Check back to v8 if you're not sure.*)

DAY 47
What do you want?

KEYPOINT
Things on earth don't last—but following Jesus is like storing up treasure in heaven.

Today's passages are:
Table Talk: Matthew 6v19-21
XTB: Matthew 6v19-34

 Treasure Hunt: Hide a few coins. Give clues to find each one. e.g. "Brr— I'm cold" (in the fridge), "Warm and cosy" (in a bed), "Brring Brring" (under the phone)

 In today's part of the Sermon on the Mount, Jesus is teaching about *treasure*. **Read Matthew 6v19-21**

 Jesus calls the things that we want <u>most</u> our **treasures**. What's the problem with storing things up on earth, such as money or possessions? (v19) *(They get destroyed and stolen)* Things on earth don't last— but where does treasure last for ever? (v20) *(Heaven)* How do we store up treasure in heaven? *(Following Jesus, living the way He wants us to, is like putting treasure into a box in heaven where we can enjoy it for ever. That's the "treasure" we should really want.)*
Read 1 Timothy 6v17-19, and think what you're going to do with those coins!

Read Matthew 6v21 aloud. Ask God to forgive you for making other things more important than Him. Ask God to help you to put Him <u>first</u>.

PRAY

Building up
Jesus goes on to explain why we shouldn't worry about possessions. **Read Matthew 6v25-34** Who and what does God provide for in these verses? *(Birds, flowers, grass, and us!)* Is God able to provide for all our needs?—v30 *(Yes!)* We know God takes care of His <u>creation</u>. It isn't logical to think He won't take care of His <u>children</u>! So ask Him to help you to trust Him and not to worry.

DAY 48
Don't judge

KEYPOINT
Don't judge others. We must remember that we disobey God too.

Today's passages are:
Table Talk: Matthew 7v3-5
XTB: Matthew 7v1-5

 Take it in turns to hold something **BIG** in front of your eyes (a piece of wood if possible, otherwise a book). Then try something fiddly like tying a bow, or drawing a picture.

 Jesus told an odd story about someone with a **log** in their eye! He used it to tell His followers <u>not to judge others</u>.
Read Matthew 7v3-5

 Think about the person in v3. What <u>does</u> he notice? *(The speck in his friend's eye)* What <u>doesn't</u> he notice? *(The plank in his own eye!)* What does he need to do <u>before</u> he can help his friend? (v5) *(Take the plank out of his eye!)*

 This story is about <u>not judging</u> others. What do you think it means? *(It's easy to point the finger at others, and not notice our own faults! We must remember that <u>we</u> disobey God too—and that He's forgiven us loads.)*

 Ask God to help you not to think you're better than others.

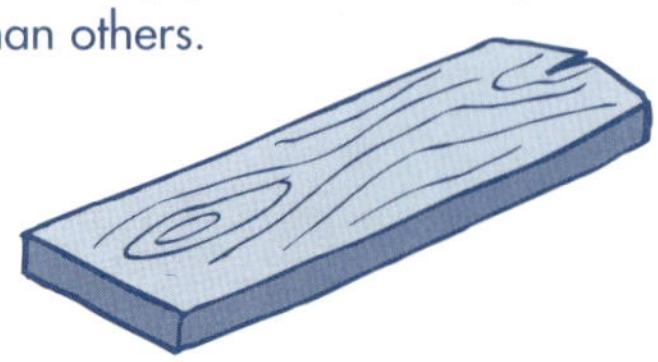

Building up
Read Matthew 7v1-2
Jesus isn't saying that it's wrong to have law courts and judges. He's saying "Don't be judgmental". **Think carefully:** How can you help your Christian friends (and yourself!) to live for God, without falling into the trap of judging them?

DAY 49
Get help!

KEYPOINT
God is our perfect heavenly Father. He will give us good gifts when we ask Him to.

Today's passages are:
Table Talk: Matthew 7v9-11
XTB: Matthew 7v7-11

Note: You need paper and pencil.

Jesus is teaching His followers about God's answers to prayer.
Read Matthew 7v9-11

What does the boy ask for? (*bread and fish*)

Draw the bread—not a modern sliced loaf, but a small flat round loaf of barley bread. **Draw the fish**—a long thin fish.

What could the father give his son instead of bread and fish? (*stone and snake*) **Draw the stone** (flat and round) **and the snake.**

What have you noticed about these pictures? (*hopefully they look similar!*) If this boy was very young, his father could trick him. Instead of giving **good** gifts, he could give **harmful** things instead. Human dads are not perfect—but they wouldn't do this!! God is our perfect heavenly Father. Will He trick us? (*No! We can trust God to give us good gifts.*)

Thank God for giving us **good** gifts.

Building up
Read Matthew 7v7-8 Jesus promises that God will always answer our prayers. Does this mean He will always give us exactly what we ask for? (*No! Sometimes we will ask for things that are not good—just as a child may ask a parent for something harmful.*) Thank God that He knows what is good, and only gives us what is good.

DAY 50
Choose wisely

KEYPOINT
Hearing Jesus' words, but not obeying Him, is as foolish as building your house on sand.

Today's passages are:
Table Talk: Matthew 7v24-27
XTB: Matthew 7v24-29

(*You need pen, paper and sticky tack.*) Draw a house on a small piece of paper. How easily can you blow it off the table? Now use sticky tack (or a weight) to hold it down. How much sticky tack or weight will stop it blowing away? (*Feeling adventurous? Then make a house from a small box and blow it with a hair dryer!*)

Jesus ended the Sermon on the Mount with a story about houses. *Or was it?*
Read Matthew 7v24-27

Where did the wise man build his house? (*On rock*) Who is like this wise man? (*Those who hear Jesus' words and obey Him*) Where did the foolish man choose? (*Sand*) Who is like him? (*Those who hear Jesus' words but don't obey Him*)

The two houses would look identical. Were they? (*No!*) People who hear Jesus' words can look identical too. But what's the difference? (*Whether they obey Jesus or not*) Can people see that difference in **you**? Have you been obeying the Sermon on the Mount as well as hearing it? How?

Ask God to help you to **do** what Jesus says.

Building up
Read Matthew 7v28-29 Why were the crowds so amazed? (v29) The religious leaders used to quote each other or the Old Testament. Jesus had His own authority. Why? (*Because of who He is.*)

DAY 51-65
Notes for Parents

GENESIS
We're returning now to **Genesis**—the **Book of Beginnings**. We've already read about the beginnings of the *universe*, and the beginnings of the *human race*. In chapter 12, Genesis starts to tell us about the beginnings of God's special family, the **Israelites**.

It begins with just three people:

SARAI
(later called Sarah)

Abram's wife

65 years old

Has never been able to have children—and now she's too old.

ABRAM
(later called Abraham)

75 years old

The Bible called Abram a **friend of God**.

LOT
Abram's nephew

Lot's father died, so Lot lived with Abram and Sarai. He was good at getting into trouble!

Map of Canaan and the countries around it at the time of Abram — about 4000 years ago.

DAY 51
Get up and go!

> **KEYPOINT**
> God promised Abram a huge family, and that all people would be blessed through Abram's family.

Today's passages are:
Table Talk: Genesis 12v1-3
XTB: Genesis 12v1-9

TABLE TALK: We're going to start finding out about a special family today, called the **Israelites**. It begins with just three people. Find out about them in **Notes for Parents** on the previous page.

READ: God gave Abram some incredible promises. **Read Genesis 12v1-3**

TALK: What did God tell Abram to do? (v1) (*Get up and go!*) God's promises were **amazing**. What would Abram's family become? (v2) (*A great nation—enough people to fill a whole country!*) Who would be blessed through Abram and his family? (v3) (*All people—including us!*)

DO: Abram, Sarai and Lot travelled a long way. Draw their route on the map on the previous page. They went from **Ur** to **Haran** to **Canaan**. (*Their journey is in Genesis 11v31 + 12v4-5*)

PRAY: Abram left everything, and went where God sent him. Ask God to help you to trust Him as much as Abram did.

Building up
Read Genesis 12v6-9 Abram travelled throughout Canaan. What did God promise him? (*To give this land to Abram's family*) Over 600 years later, Joshua led more than two million members of Abram's family back into the land of Canaan. (*See Joshua 1v6*) By then Abram's family were called the **Israelites**, and the land was renamed **Israel**. God had kept His promises.

DAY 52 To and Fro? Yes and no!

> **KEYPOINT**
> Abram let God down. He fled to Egypt and lied about Sarai. But God didn't let Abram down!

Today's passages are:
Table Talk: Genesis 12v17-20
XTB: Genesis 12v10-20

TABLE TALK: God brought Abram to Canaan and made him some amazing promises. But when a famine hit Canaan, there was very little food to eat—so Abram decided to go to Egypt instead. **Draw his journey on yesterday's map.**

READ: Abram's wife Sarai was very beautiful. Abram was worried that someone would **kill** him so that they could marry Sarai—so he told her to pretend she was his **sister**! When Pharaoh, the king of Egypt, heard how beautiful Sarai was he thought she was Abram's sister, so he took her to his palace to be his wife! **Read Genesis 12v17-20**

TALK: What happened to Pharaoh and those in his palace? (v17) (*God made them ill*) When Pharaoh found out who Sarai really was, what did he do? (v20) (*Sent Abram and Sarai back to Canaan*) **Draw their journey back on the map.**

THINK: Abram let God down. He fled to Egypt and lied about Sarai. But God **didn't** let Abram down! He brought him safely back to Canaan. We **all** let God down sometimes—but God **never** lets us down!

PRAY: Thank God that He is like this.

Building up
As Abram discovered, even when we are faithless, God is <u>always</u> faithful—He never lets us down.
Read 2 Timothy 2v13
Thank God that He is like this.

DAY 53
What a Lot!

KEYPOINT
Abram and Lot split up to have more room. Lot made the foolish choice to live near wicked Sodom

Today's passages are:
Table Talk: Genesis 13v10-13
XTB: Genesis 13v1-13

TABLE TALK
All sit on **one** chair! Are you comfortable? Who's feeling squashed? Could you stay like that for a whole meal??

READ
In today's story, Abram and his nephew Lot are feeling squashed! They both have lots of sheep and goats and cows and camels... There isn't enough grass for them to stay together. So Abram decides they must split, and gives Lot first choice of where to go.
Read Genesis 13v10-13

TALK
Lot could choose the beautiful Jordan valley, or the hills of Canaan. Which did he choose? (v11) (*Jordan valley*) Where did Lot live? (v12) (*Near Sodom*)

Lot's choice may have been **selfish**—the Jordan valley was easier to farm than the hill. But it was also a **foolish** choice. Why? (See v13) (*He was living near Sodom, where the people didn't care about God or His laws*) We'll see the result of Lot's foolish choice in chapter 14.

PRAY
Ask God to help you to make **wise** choices—not foolish or selfish ones.

Building up
(*Mainly for older children.*) Lot was unwise to live so near to Sodom. Can you think of people or places you would be <u>wise</u> to avoid? (*E.g. friends who have started shoplifting or trying out Tarot Cards; or parties where people think it's cool to get drunk or take drugs*)

DAY 54
A dusty promise

KEYPOINT
God made HUGE promises to Abram—huge amounts of land and a huge family.

Today's passages are:
Table Talk: Genesis 14v14-16
XTB: Genesis 14v14-18

TABLE TALK
Pile something small onto a plate. (*Sand, rice, lentils...*) Now try to count them!

READ
Lot and Abram had split the land between them. Lot chose the Jordan valley to farm in. Abram was left with the hills of Canaan. It <u>looked</u> like Abram had lost out—but see what God promised him... **Read Genesis 13v14-16**

TALK
Where did God tell Abram to look? (v14) (*In <u>all</u> directions*) How much land did God promise to give Abram and his family? (v15) (*All of it!*) How big would Abram's family become? (v16) (*Too big to count—like counting dust, or lentils!*)

THINK
God's promises to Abram were HUGE! **Huge** amounts of land. A **huge** family. God gives <u>us</u> huge promises too. Can you think of any? (*E.g. To love us, to listen when we pray, to be with us all the time, to forgive our sins because of Jesus...*)

PRAY
Thank God for His huge promises to you.

Building up
Over 600 years later, Moses counted up the Israelites.
Read Numbers 26v1-2 + 51

Moses <u>only</u> counted the men who were the right age to join the army. (More than 600,000 of them!) If you add everyone else as well, there were between 2 and 3 million Israelites!! God certainly kept His promise to Abram!

DAY 55 The battle of the kings

> **KEYPOINT**
> Lot moved into Sodom, and was captured in a battle. God helped Abram to rescue him.

Today's passages are:
Table Talk: Genesis 14v14-16
XTB: Genesis 14v1-20

TABLE TALK

(You need 2 pieces of paper. Draw 4 crowns on one, and a stick man (Lot) on the other. You also need 5 objects to be cities. e.g. saucers)

DO

Lay out the five cities. Choose one to be Sodom. What was the <u>foolish</u> choice Lot had made? (13v12—to live near Sodom) **Put the stick man near to Sodom.** BUT Lot then moved <u>into</u> Sodom. **Put Lot into the city.** 4 powerful kings (**move 4 crowns**) came to attack the 5 cities in the Jordan valley. They defeated Sodom (**turn the saucer over**) and captured everyone living there, including Lot and his family. **Move 4 crowns and Lot away from the cities.** One man escaped, and ran to find Abram. **Read Genesis 14v14-16**

READ

TALK

What did Abram do? (Abram attacked at night, defeated the 4 kings and brought Lot safely home.) **Move Lot back near to Sodom.**

How many men did Abram have? (v14) (318) Was this enough men to defeat 4 powerful kings? (No!) So why did Abram win? (Check your answer in v20)

PRAY

It <u>looked</u> impossible—but **God** was on Abram's side! Thank God that nothing is impossible for Him.

Building up
Are you worried about anything at the moment? Remember that **nothing** is too big or too difficult for God (see Luke 1v37). Ask Him to help you.

DAY 56 Meet Melchizedek

> **KEYPOINT**
> After rescuing Lot, Abram gave a tenth of everything to God by giving it to God's priest, Melchizedek.

Today's passages are:
Table Talk: Genesis 14v17-20
XTB: Genesis 14v17-24

TABLE TALK

Recap: Retell the story of Lot being captured by the 4 kings, then rescued by Abram.

When Abram and Lot returned, they were met by the king of Sodom, (where Lot had been living), and by another king who had a very long name...
Read Genesis 14v17-20

READ

TALK

Who were the two kings who met Abram? (The kings of Sodom and Salem [Jerusalem]) Melchizedek was a **Priest** as well as a **King**. What did he give Abram? (v18+19) (Bread and wine, and his blessing) What did Abram give Melchizedek? (v20) (A tenth of everything he'd captured from the 4 kings)

THINK

The king of Sodom wanted Abram to keep some of the loot from Sodom—but Abram refused to keep even a thread! He didn't want his wealth to come from such an evil king. (See v23) Abram knew that **everything** he had came from God. He gave a <u>tenth</u> back to God by giving it to God's priest, Melchizedek.

PRAY

Everything <u>you</u> have comes from God. What will you give back to Him? (Your time? Your abilities? Your...?) Pray about your answers.

Building up
Melchizedek suddenly pops up in this story, then goes again. We know almost nothing about him. But the NT says he points forward to the only perfect King and Priest—**Jesus**. (See Hebrews 7v1-3)

DAY 57
Seeing stars

KEYPOINT
God again promised Abram a son—and that his family would be as many as the stars in the sky.

Today's passages are:
Table Talk: Genesis 15v4-6
XTB: Genesis 15v1-6

DO
Draw a circle on some paper. Ask everyone to draw lots of stars round the circle. Write **"God is the Star-Maker"** inside the circle (*leave space underneath for some more writing.*).

READ

(illustration of a circle surrounded by stars, with "God is the Star-Maker" written inside)

Abram was worried because he and Sarai still didn't have any children. It looked like one of Abram's **servants** would inherit everything.
Read Genesis 15v4-6

TALK
What did God promise Abram? (*That Abram's own son would be his heir*) What did God tell Abram to look at? (v5) (*The stars*) What did Abram do? (v6) (*He believed God*)

Abram <u>believed</u> that God would keep His promise. Write **"God is the Promise Keeper"** in the circle on your sheet of paper.

PRAY
When you pray, you are talking to God the Star-Maker and Promise-Keeper. How does that make you feel? Talk to God about it.

Building up
Read Genesis 1v16 Abram was looking up at the stars that **God** had made. Do you think God the Star-Maker was <u>able</u> to keep His promise to Abram? Why?

DAY 58
God's friends

KEYPOINT
Abram believed God—and God accepted Him. Abram's faith made him right with God.

Today's passages are:
Table Talk: Genesis 15v6
XTB: Genesis 15v6

TABLE TALK
Each think of one friend. Say who they are and why they are a good friend.

READ
The Bible calls Abram a **"friend of God"** (James 2v23) But we know that Abram <u>sinned</u>—and that sin <u>stops</u> people from being God's friends. So <u>why</u> was Abram called God's friend?
Read Genesis 15v6 to find out.

TALK
What did Abram do? (*He believed/ trusted God*) What did God do? (*He accepted Abram as <u>righteous</u>—that means being <u>right</u> with God*)

THINK
Abram **believed** God—and God **accepted** him. Abram didn't have to keep lots of rules, or live a perfect life. He **trusted** God's promises, and that made him **right** with God. He was God's friend.

(*You need pencil and paper.*) Look back to **Notes for Parents** on **Day 7**. Follow the ideas outlined there to remind each other how Jesus' death makes it possible for <u>us</u> to be God's friends too.

PRAY
Thank God for sending Jesus so that you can be His friends.

Building up
In Romans 4, Paul uses the example of Abram to explain that being made right with God has <u>always</u> been through faith. **Read Romans 4v18-24** Like Abram, it is through <u>faith</u> that <u>we</u> are put right with God (v24).

DAY 59
Coming in to land

KEYPOINT
God promised to give Canaan to Abram's family. God always keeps His promises.

Today's passages are:
Table Talk: Genesis 15v13-16
XTB: Genesis 15v7-21

TABLE TALK

(*You need pen and paper.*) Copy these sentences onto 3 pieces of paper.
A: Abram died peacefully when he was 175 years old. (*Genesis 25v7-8*)
B: Abram's family, the Israelites, were slaves in Egypt for 400 years (*Exodus 2v23-24*)
C: God chose Moses to lead the Israelites out of Egypt. (*Exodus 3v15-17*)

READ

God promised to give the land of Canaan to Abram's family. He also told Abram what would happen in the future... **Read Genesis 15v13-16 slowly**, stopping each time that God's promise matches sentence A, B or C.

(*Optional*) Look up these verses to see how God's promises were kept.
A=Genesis 25v7-8; **B**=Exodus 2v23-24; **C**=Exodus 3v15-17

PRAY

All through the Bible we see that God is both Promise-Giver and Promise-Keeper. God never makes a promise that He can't keep! Thank God for being like this.

Building up
The details of God's covenant (binding agreement) with Abram seem a bit odd! When people made covenants in those days, they'd kill some animals or birds, then walk between the dead bodies! That's what **v7-11** and **v17-21** are all about. God was showing Abram that He would keep His covenant promises.

DAY 60
Waiting for God

KEYPOINT
Abram and Sarai had a son through Sarai's servant, Hagar. But he wasn't the son God had promised.

Today's passages are:
Table Talk: Genesis 16v7-10
XTB: Genesis 16v1-16

TABLE TALK

What do you find it hard to wait for? (*A holiday, exam results, Christmas, for a loose baby tooth to fall out...*) Abram and Sarai waited **10 years** for God to give them a son. Then they tried to fix the problem themselves...

READ

Sarai told Abram to take her servant Hagar as his second wife. That way Abram could have a son. Abram agreed, but after Hagar became pregnant she began to look down on Sarai. Sarai then started to treat Hagar badly—so Hagar ran away. **Read Genesis 16v7-10**

TALK

Who met Hagar in the desert? (v7) (*The angel of the Lord—speaking God's message*) What did he tell Hagar to do? (v9) (*Go back to Sarai*) What did he promise Hagar? (v10) (*She would have a huge family*)

THINK

Hagar's son, Ishmael, was the start of a huge family—just as God had promised. God is always faithful.

But Ishmael wasn't the son Abram and Sarai had been told to wait for. They still had to wait **much longer** for him. Ask God to help you to trust Him, and to wait patiently.

PRAY

Building up
Sometimes it's very hard to trust that God will do what's best for us. Instead, we want to make things happen on our own. Think of one way that you're tempted to abandon what God has said and to do your own thing. Pray about it, asking God to help you to trust Him.

DAY 61
New names

KEYPOINT
God gave Abram and Sarai new names—Abraham and Sarah. And again promised to give them a son.

Today's passages are:
Table Talk: Genesis 17v3-6;15;21
XTB: Genesis 17v1-27

TABLE TALK Talk about your names. Do you like them? Would you change your name? What to?

READ Imagine changing your name when you're 99! That's how old Abram was when God appeared to Him and gave him a new name. **Read Gen 17v3-6**

TALK What was Abram's new name? (*Abraham*) Abraham means "father of many". Why was this a good name for him? (v6) (*He would be the start of a huge family*) What new thing did God say about Abraham's family? (*Some would be kings*)

Sarai was given a new name too. **Read Genesis 17v15** What was her new name? (*Sarah—both Sarai and Sarah mean "princess"*)

God also renewed His promise to give Abraham and Sarah a son. He was to be called *Isaac*. **Read Genesis 17v21** When would Isaac be born? (*In a year's time*)

PRAY It had been a long wait—but the time had now come for God to keep His promise. Thank God that He <u>always</u> keeps His promises.

Building up
God told Abraham that he and his family were to be **circumcised** (a small piece of skin cut off from their penises). This would be a sign of God's covenant promises to them. **Read Genesis 17v9-11** As soon as God stopped speaking to Abraham, he and his family were all circumcised, just as God said (v23-27).

DAY 62
Three strangers

KEYPOINT
Three strangers visited Abraham and Sarah to tell Abraham that Sarah would soon have a son.

Today's passages are:
Table Talk: Genesis 18v9-15
XTB: Genesis 18v1-15

TABLE TALK Talk about any visitors you've had recently. Who were your favourites? How did you show you were pleased to see them?

READ Three visitors turned up unexpectedly at Abraham's tent. As Abraham soon realised, two of them were angels. The other one was **God**! Abraham ran to make them a special meal. Then he waited nearby, under a tree.
Read Genesis 18v9-15

TALK What did God say would happen in a year's time? (v10) (*He would return, and Sarah would have a son*)
Why did Sarah laugh? (*She knew she was far too old to have a baby*)
What did God remind Abraham and Sarah about? (v14) (*Nothing is too hard for God*)

DO (*Optional*) Copy v14 **"Is anything too hard for the Lord?"** onto a sheet. Decorate it, and stick it to the wall to remind you that God can do **anything**.

PRAY Thank God that <u>nothing</u> is too hard for Him.

Building up
Read v15 God knew what Sarah was thinking—even when she tried to lie about it. God knows everything **we** think and say and do—even when no-one else does. **Think carefully:** *adults as well as children.* Is there anything you need to say sorry to God about? Ask Him to forgive you, and to help you to trust and obey Him.

DAY 63
A son is born

KEYPOINT
God kept His promise to give Abraham and Sarah a son. He was called Isaac.

Today's passages are:
Table Talk: Genesis 21v5-7
XTB: Genesis 21v1-7

TABLE TALK

What makes you laugh? (*Jokes, happy memories, watching a little child...*)

Why did Sarah laugh in yesterday's story? (*She thought she was too old to have the child God had promised*) In today's story we're skipping ahead a few chapters. A year has gone past, and God has kept His promise. Sarah has had a son, called **Isaac**. His name means "*He laughs*"
Read Genesis 21v5-7

TALK

Sarah was 90 years old when Isaac was born. How old was Abraham? (v5) (*100!*) Why did Sarah laugh this time? (v6) (*She laughed for joy*)

Sarah laughed with delight because God had kept His promise to her. God is the Promise-Keeper. He <u>always</u> keeps His promises. How can you show **your** delight? (*By praying? Making something? Telling someone else? Laughing?...*)

PRAY

Choose one way to thank and praise God for being the Promise-Keeper.

Building up
Read Genesis 21v1-4

How many times do these verses say that something happened just as **God had said**? Why do you think the writer of Genesis keeps repeating this? What does He want us to understand about God? (*God's purposes always come about. God's words will always come true.*)

DAY 64-65
Notes for Parents

ABRAHAM SACRIFICING ISAAC
God tested Abraham by telling him to sacrifice his son Isaac. This was a very hard test for Abraham to take—and very hard for children (and us!) to understand. The following explanations should help:

SACRIFICES
Abraham would be used to making **sacrifices**. He would kill an animal or bird, burn it, & offer it to God. It was a way of saying sorry or thank you to God.

This was a huge test. Abraham loved Isaac. He also knew that God's promise of a huge family started with Isaac. But Abraham had faith in God—and because he trusted God, he also obeyed Him. (*Note: Nobody else in the Bible was asked to do this. Your children don't need to be worried!*)

SUBSTITUTE
A substitute is a familiar idea from team games. When a football or rugby player is injured, someone else comes on <u>in their place</u>. They are the **substitute**.

JESUS—OUR SACRIFICE AND SUBSTITUTE
John the Baptist once said about Jesus: **"Look, the Lamb of God, who takes away the sin of the world!"** *John 1v29*

When Jesus died, He was being **sacrificed**. His death was the punishment for our sin. He died in our place, as our **substitute**. This was how Jesus fulfilled God's promise to Abraham, that one of Abraham's family would be God's way of blessing the whole world. (Genesis 22v18)

DAY 64
The toughest test

KEYPOINT
God tested Abraham by telling him to sacrifice his son Isaac. Abraham was ready to obey God, but God stopped him.

Today's passages are:
Table Talk: Genesis 22v1-2, 11-12
XTB: Genesis 22v1-14

TABLE TALK

Note: Please read **Notes for Parents** first. (You need pen & paper.) Play hangman with the words SACRIFICE and SUBSTITUTE.

READ

These two words are key to understanding this last story about Abraham. **Read Genesis 22v1-2**

TALK

What was God doing? (v1) (*Testing Abraham*) What did God tell Abraham to do? (*Sacrifice Isaac*)

It was a very hard test, but Abraham did what God said. He and Isaac went to the mountain God showed them. Then Abraham took his son and lifted his knife, ready to kill Isaac. But God <u>stopped</u> him. **Read Genesis 22v11-12**

What did God tell Abraham? (v12) (*Not to hurt Isaac*) Abraham had shown that he loved God **more** than anything else. He was ready to kill his own son—but God stopped him, and provided a ram to be the sacrifice instead (v13). The ram was a **substitute** for Isaac—it died in his place. (*More about that tomorrow.*)

See **Building Up** for prayer ideas.

Building up
The Bible says we should love God **more** than anyone else. This doesn't mean you stop loving your family. In fact, God will help you to love them even more than you do now! But it does mean that God will be the most important person in your life. Do you want to love God this much? Ask Him to help you.

DAY 65
Substitute

KEYPOINT
A ram was sacrificed instead of Isaac. In the same way, Jesus died in our place, as our substitute.

Today's passages are:
Table Talk: Genesis 22v13-14, 18
XTB: Genesis 22v15-19

TABLE TALK

Recap: Retell the story of God telling Abraham to sacrifice Isaac. Recap the meanings of *sacrifice* and *substitute*.

READ

God stopped Abraham from killing Isaac, but the sacrifice still had to be made...
Read Genesis 22v13-14

TALK

What was sacrificed instead of Isaac? (*A ram*) The ram died in Isaac's place. It was a **substitute**. After the sacrifice, God repeated His promises to Abraham. He again said that one of Abraham's family would be God's way of blessing the whole world.
Read Genesis 22v18

THINK

Jesus came from Abraham's family! God kept His promise to Abraham by sending Jesus to be our **substitute**. Jesus died in our place, so that we can be forgiven and can be friends with God. (See **Notes for Parents** for a fuller explanation.)

PRAY

Thank God for sending Jesus as <u>your</u> substitute.

Building up
Chapter 11 of Hebrews lists people of faith from the Old Testament. **Read Hebrews 11v11-12 + 17-19** to see what it says about Abraham. What have <u>you</u> learnt from Abraham? Ask God to help you to trust and obey Him as Abraham did.

Extra Readings

WHY ARE THERE EXTRA READINGS?

Table Talk and **XTB** both come out every three months. The main Bible reading pages contain material for 65 days. That's enough to use them Monday to Friday for three months.

Many families find that their routine is different at weekends from during the week. Some find that regular Bible reading fits in well on school days, but not at weekends. Others encourage their children to read the Bible for themselves during the week, then explore the Bible together as a family at weekends, when there's more time to do the activities together.

The important thing is to help your children get into the habit of reading for the Bible for themselves—and that they see that regular Bible reading is important for **you** as well.

If you **are** able to read the Bible with your children every day, that's great! The extra readings on the next page will augment the main **Table Talk** pages so that you have enough material to cover the full three months.

You could:

- Read **Table Talk** every day for 65 days, then use the extra readings for the rest of the third month.

- Read **Table Talk** on weekdays. Use the extra readings at weekends.

- Use any other combination that works for your family.

WHAT IS GOD LIKE?

The book of Genesis has helped us to find out what God is like. In these extra readings we're going to see what some other parts of the Bible say about **God's character.**

There are 26 Bible readings on the next page. Part of each verse has been printed for you—but with a word missing. Fill in the missing words as you read the verses. Then see if you can find them all in the wordsearch.

Note: Some are written backwards—or diagonally!!

M	S	N	N	D	M	S	S	I	C	H	A	N	G	E
E	N	S	E	G	Y	P	T	V	D	O	O	G	C	S
R	O	A	D	X	S	R	E	H	T	O	M	A	D	O
C	T	E	T	R	V	E	S	E	G	R	F	R	V	S
Y	H	B	D	F	O	S	H	F	T	U	O	S	I	C
F	I	R	E	A	A	W	E	R	O	W	O	N	D	A
Y	N	H	E	A	R	T	P	V	S	R	N	H	O	R
T	G	S	E	H	N	K	H	T	E	E	G	B	T	E
H	P	R	O	M	I	S	E	E	R	I	B	I	V	R
G	L	O	R	Y	A	A	R	S	R	T	L	I	V	S
R	G	R	S	S	R	N	D	G	O	D	S	E	R	E
E	V	O	L	S	S	E	N	D	O	O	G	S	B	B

Extra Readings

1 ☐ Read Exodus 20v1-6
God reminded the Israelites of all that He had done for them.
"I am the LORD your God who brought you out of E _ _ _ _ where you were slaves." (v2)

2 ☐ Read Deuteronomy 4v23-24
Moses warned the Israelites not to follow pretend gods.
"The Lord your God is like a flaming f _ _ _ ." (v24)

3 ☐ Read Deuteronomy 10v17-22
Moses reminded the Israelites that God is fair and just.
"God does not show partiality, and he does not accept b _ _ _ _ _ _ ." (v17)

4 ☐ Read Joshua 23v14-16
Joshua reminded the Israelites that God keep His promises.
"Every p _ _ _ _ _ _ _ God made has been kept; not one has failed." (v14)

5 ☐ Read 1 Samuel 16v6-7
God told Samuel what kind of king He was looking for.
"Man looks at the outward appearance, but God looks at the h _ _ _ _ ." (v7)

6 ☐ Read 1Samuel 17v41-47
David told Goliath why God would help him to beat the huge Philistine.
"The whole world will know that Israel has a God, and everyone here will see that the LORD does not need s _ _ _ _ _ _ or spears to save his people." (v46-47)

7 ☐ Read Psalm 19v1-6
Psalm 19 shows how the world points us to God our Creator.
"How clearly the sky reveals God's g _ _ _ _ _ ." (v1)

8 ☐ Read Psalm 23v1-4
David (who was a shepherd himself) wrote a song about God being a shepherd too.
"The LORD is my s _ _ _ _ _ _ _ _ : I have everything I need." (v1)

9 ☐ Read Psalm 23v5-6
The second half of David's song about God our Shepherd…
"I know that your g _ _ _ _ _ _ _ _ and love will be with me all my life." (v6)

10 ☐ Read Psalm 33v1-5
This psalm shows that what God says always comes true.
"The W _ _ _ _ of the LORD are true and all his works are dependable." (v4)

Extra Readings

11 ☐ **Read Psalm 51v1-9**
David's song about God's compassion and mercy.
"Have m _ _ _ _ on me, O God, because of your constant love. Because of your great mercy wipe away my sins!" (v1)

12 ☐ **Read Psalm 65v9-13**
David writes about how God looks after our world.
"You show your c _ _ _ for the land by sending rain; you make it rich and fertile." (v9)

13 ☐ **Read Psalm 106v1-3**
A long psalm, thanking God for His goodness to the Israelites.
"Give thanks to the LORD, because he is g _ _ _ ; his love is eternal."(v1)

14 ☐ **Read Psalm 139v1-6**
This psalm shows us how much God knows about us.
"You know everything I do; from far away you understand all my t _ _ _ _ _ _ _ ." (v2)

15 ☐ **Read Psalm 139v7-12**
Everywhere we go, God can see us and help us.
"Even darkness is not d _ _ _ for you." (v12)

16 ☐ **Read Psalm 139v13-18**
God knew all about you before you were even born!
"You created every part of me; you put me together in my m _ _ _ _ _ ' _ womb." (v13)

17 ☐ **Read Isaiah 40v25-26**
Isaiah reminds his readers that God is the one who made and knows each star.
"He calls each star by n _ _ _ ." (v26)

18 ☐ **Read Malachi 3v6**
Malachi (the last book in the Old Testament) tells us that God always stays the same.
"I am the LORD, and I do not c _ _ _ _ _ _ ." (v6)

19 ☐ **Read Luke 1v35-38**
The angel Gabriel tells Mary that God can do anything.
"For n _ _ _ _ _ _ _ is impossible with God—there is nothing that God cannot do." (v37)

20 ☐ **Read John 3v16-17**
John tells us why God sent His Son Jesus to die for us.
"For God loved the world so much that he gave his only Son, so that everyone who b _ _ _ _ _ _ _ in him may not die but have eternal life." (v16)

Extra Readings

21 ☐ Read John 14v8-11
Philip asked Jesus to show him what God is like. Jesus said:
"Whoever has seen me has seen the F _ _ _ _ _ ." (v9)

22 ☐ Read Romans 5v6-11
Paul's letter to Christians in Rome shows us how much God loves us.
"But God has shown us how much he loves us—it was while we were still S _ _ _ _ _ _ that Christ died for us!" (v8)

23 ☐ Read 1 John 1v8-10
John reminds us that we sin—and need to ask God to forgive us.
"If we confess our sins to God ... he will f _ _ _ _ _ _ us our sins." (v9)

24 ☐ Read 1 John 4v7-10
John goes on to say that we know that God loves us because He sent Jesus to die for us.
"God is l _ _ _ ." (v8)

25 ☐ Read Revelation 21v1-4
The book of Revelation ends with a picture of what heaven will be like.
"God will wipe away all t _ _ _ _ from their eyes. There will be no more death, no more grief or crying or pain." (v4)

26 ☐ Read Revelation 21v22-27
Heaven is like a city—with no need for sun or moon because God is its light.
"The city has no need of the sun or the moon to shine on it, because the glory of G _ _ shines on it, and the Lamb is its lamp." (v23)

WHAT NEXT?

We hope that **Table Talk** has helped you get into a regular habit of reading the Bible with your children.

Table Talk comes out every three months. Each issue contains 65 full **Table Talk** outlines, plus 26 days of extra readings. By the time you've used them all, the next issue will be available.

Available from your local Christian bookshop—or call us on **020 8942 0880** to order a copy.

COMING SOON!
Issue Two: Miracles and Dreams

Issue Two of Table Talk carries on in the books of Genesis, Matthew and Acts. It dips into the book of Psalms as well.

- Meet Jacob the Schemer and Joseph the Dreamer in the book of **Genesis**.
- Investigate Jesus' miracles in **Matthew's** Gospel.
- Discover why Peter's dream changed everything for the first Christians as you read more of the book of **Acts**.